LIONEL MARTIN
a biography

LIONEL MARTIN
a biography

by
A.B Demaus

TRANSPORT BOOKMAN PUBLICATIONS

ISBN 0 85184 032 9

Cover design by
David Harris

Design and layout by
Barbara and David Harris

Typeset by
Wordplay (Test Processors) Limited,
Hounslow, England

Printed in Great Britain by
R. J. Acford Limited, Chichester

CONTENTS

ACKNOWLEDGEMENTS

The author is very greatly indebted to so many people and institutions for help in the production of this book, for it is abundantly true to say that had it not been for their unstinting help and advice it could not have been written. The passing of the years since Lionel Martin's death in 1945 has taken so many of his friends and contemporaries who might well have enabled the author to produce a deeper and broader portrait of the man and his cars; all the more gratitude, therefore, to those who have so generously helped the author in his task.

(The late) Lt-Colonel Charles Archdale
L. Baker, Esq.
M.W.N. Bancroft, Esq.
P.T. Beardsell, Esq.
W. Boddy, Esq.
Lt-Colonel C.E. Bowden
R. Dallas Brett, Esq., OBE
A.W. Bush, Esq.
E.R. Cass, Esq.
J.I. Cheyne, Esq.
H.G. Conway, Esq.
The Editor, *Motor Boat & Yachting*
S.C.H. Davis, Esq.
J.O. Dyson, Esq.
(The late) F.E. Ellis, Esq.
(The late) Capt. G.E.T. Eyston, OBE, MC
G.N. Georgano, Esq.
Mrs. A.G. Gripper
Gwent County Council: the County Archivist
J.D. Hall, Esq.
W.D. Hall, Esq.
E. Inman Hunter, Esq.
D. Irvine, Esq.

L.O. James, Esq.
Lt-Colonel R.A.C. Jennings, MBE, DL
Count Johnston Noad
R.J.H. Kay, Esq.
E.M. Lea-Major, Esq
John Martin, Esq.
S. Maslin, Esq.
Mrs Marion Morgan
(The late) R.C. Morgan, Esq.
Neil F. Murray, Esq.
D.A. Paine, Esq.
H.G. Pitt, Esq.
Mrs. Jean K. Rawson
John Stanford, Esq.
Dr. Patrick Strong
Thomas of Remenham, DFC, The Lord
D.B. Tubbs, Esq.
J.B. Turner, Esq.
P.J. Wallace, Esq.
E.J. Warburton, Esq.
Capt. The Revd H. Ward
S.D. Wicks, Esq.
The Aston Martin Owners Club, and in particular John Classey
    and Tony Byles
The Bath Road Club and its Officers, particularly J. Aston
    and T.D. Passmore
The Brooklands Society, and in particular their Archivist,
    Walter Gibbs Esq.
The Midland Automobile Club, and in particular their Archivist,
    Walter Gibbs Esq.

FOREWORD

When Mr Demaus told me of his plan to write a biography of my Father I liked the idea and was even more attracted to it when I met the author and heard of his life-long and close interest in the Bamford and Martin cars and his sympathetic insight into the subject and his immediate circle. I feel there should certainly be a written memorial to my Father as his contribution to motor sport may well have been overlooked and not fully appreciated.

It says a great deal for his largeness of character that after the disappointment at the failure of his project he did not withdraw from motor sport altogether but was determined to put back into the sport as much or more than he has had from it. He was a member of the R.A.C. Competitions Committee, he seldom missed a major Brooklands meeting as one of the Stewards, acted as Official car or marshal at innumerable M.C.C. — Exeter, Land's End, and Edinburgh Trials and was often an official at the events of the Bugatti Owners Club. How enjoyable those M.C.C. events were, especially the Land's End, starting in the cold of midnight and finishing in the warm sun and Spring flowers of the West Country. The cars were nearly all completely standard and thus, in many ways, more interesting than ostensibly normal models altered out of all knowledge by the factories. I was later able to appreciate what an excellent Steward and Official my Father made. Having always had independent means he had no axe to grind and was not in the least impressed by the big names of the day and was always scrupulously fair and even-handed in the appeals and disputes that arose from time to time.

Such a Foreword is inevitably nostalgic and I was just old enough to appreciate what fun it was at "The Hollies" just off Edwardes Square. The Abingdon Road works were only a few minutes away and my parents kept open-house, and to it gravitated a great number of bright and clever young people, many of whom eventually became household names in the world of motoring. One of my earliest recollections is of Count Zborowski. I had a very pious nurse who made me say my prayers every night and somehow she

8

persuaded the Count to come and say good-night to me. I was on my knees when the visitor entered but I could appreciate the delicious contrast between the debonair and immaculate Count and the strongly disapproving nanny. Another memory is when my parents came to take me out for the day from my Surrey Prep. School in one of the long-tailed Brooklands racers sans mudguards and an open exhaust. The other boys, of course, were very impressed and jealous, not so the masters who thought me the spoiled brat of fast and rackety parents.

I remember how proud I was of the cars and this came out at a hill-climb on a public road as was then legal; it could well have been Kop. I was standing on the bank which made a natural grandstand when a marshal shouted "Stand well back......fast car coming!" and it was *Bunny* or *Razorblade*......all our cars had nicknames. I nearly burst with pride and ran from spectator to spectator yelling, "That's our car, that's our car."

One aspect of my Father's thinking on cars was that he always remained faithful to the concept of the quality small car. Even when there was a Railton in the garage he left that to my Step-mother to drive and always preferred the Lancia Aprilia or B.M.W. 327 or 328. Whilst full of admiration for the way the present management has revived the fortunes of Aston Martin, I cannot but feel he would have deplored the way the cars have got bigger and bigger over the years, and would have regarded the present products as dinosaurs. Legislation and the vagaries of the world oil situation may well prove him right.

I welcome this book, I am sure that all Aston Martin enthusiasts will enjoy it and I ardently hope that the marque will continue to prosper and carry on the name and fine tradition for craftsmanship that my Father created.

John Martin

AUTHOR'S PREFACE

Schoolmasters, it is said, have much to answer for, and certainly if the wordy outpourings of modern educational theory are anything to go by, it would seem hard to deny that there must be at least a grain of truth in this generalisation. But it is equally true that however much, as a profession, they may wish to be remembered by their teachings it is often by aspects of their behaviour or character manifested outside the classroom that they are best remembered.

In the author's case he has every cause to be grateful to a certain individual schoolmaster, not for what he learned from him in the classroom (which has long ago been lost in the limbo of time) but for the fact that he owned one of Lionel Martin's Aston-Martins, and a particularly delightful one at that. By such a whim of fortune, for, as a ten-year-old, the author was allowed to fuss over this car, to clean it and polish it lovingly for an occasional reward of, perhaps, a bar of chocolate or — much more appreciated — the privilege of a run in the car, there has been engendered in the author a lasting love of vintage motor cars, a determination to own a Lionel Martin Aston and, eventually, a burning desire to record an appreciation of Lionel Martin as a man and of his superbly high-quality cars.

Nearly twenty years after this schoolboy infatuation the author was lucky enough to acquire one of the most historic of all the products of Lionel Martin's tiny Kensington factory. This was the short-chassis Grand Prix car that had been raced with so much success by the late Robert Morgan and his wife, a car which later research revealed to be none other than the car raced by Count Zborowski in the French Grand Prix at Strasbourg in 1922 and on many other occasions.

This was followed by a touring side-valver which had been owned by racing motorist and motoring correspondent Capt. J.C. Douglas, a car which, despite its lack of racing 'glamour', gave the author many miles of delightful motoring.

Both these cars have long since left the author's ownership but the enthralling mystique of the Bamford & Martin Astons remained. In compiling this book the author has unashamedly called upon the help of very many other people who in one way or another were or are concerned with these Lionel Martin cars or — and how sadly few remain — were friends or contemporaries of Lionel and Katherine Martin at the time the cars were in production. In the *Acknowledgments* the author has tried to give credit to those who have helped in any way, and if, inadvertently, someone has been left out, the author offers sincere apologies.

It is impossible to assess just how important the contributions of any one individual or institution may have been in compiling this book; a single fact may be so vital to the whole, even if he who supplies it is unaware how vital it is, that any attempt to 'grade' such contributions would indeed be invidious. But if the author may be allowed to express his particular thanks to the following, on the basis of the degree to which he has plagued them for information, then such particular mention is fully deserved.

First, to Lionel's son, John, who has so kindly consented to write a Foreword to this book and whose first-hand knowledge and help has been quite invaluable; to the late Robert Morgan, Mrs Marion Morgan and Neil Murray, who were or are so intimately concerned with the racer 'Green Pea'; to the late F.E. Ellis for advice and help over many years; to Ted Inman Hunter whose knowledge of all the pre-David Brown Astons has been so generously shared in answer to the author's many queries; to Tony Byles of the Aston Martin Owners Club and to Jack Aston of the Bath Road Club for their part in allowing the author access to matters with which this book is concerned; and to Mrs Agnes Gripper for her invaluable help in giving a feminine view of Katherine Martin as she knew her.

Lionel Martin; a photograph taken from an oil
painting by Alan Bowyer, R.O.I.

CHAPTER ONE

Lionel Walker Birch Martin was born on 15 March 1878, son of E.M. Martin and his wife, formerly Birch, into what would be termed 'comfortable circumstances'. He entered Eton, where he was a member of Vaughan's House, in the Michaelmas Term 1891 and left at the end of the Summer Term 1896. At the time of his entry into Eton his parents' address was given as Albert Gate Mansions, Knightsbridge, London S.W.

Despite the fact that some present-day wag has said publicly that anyone who has spent five years or so at Eton has served the equivalent of a five-year prison sentence, Martin appears to have enjoyed his time there and to have retained a great pride in and affection for his old school throughout his life.

The closing decade of the nineteenth century was an exciting period for a boy of Martin's background and social standing to grow up in, and prospects must have seemed at least pleasurable, if not rosy, to this young Etonian. He could not have failed to have been influenced by the atmosphere of the time, the pleasure-seeking, the air of 'fin de siècle', the talk and pastimes of the society in which he lived. During his time at Eton 'Society' was increasingly conscious of the impact of the bicycle and by the time he left Eton in 1896 the bicycle and everything pertaining to it had become the object of a degree of acclaim so great as to constitute a 'craze' which in turn brought about a cycle 'boom' in which firms and individuals were enthusiastically, and sometimes disastrously, caught up. Indeed, the interest that 'Society' took in the pastime swelled to a torrent, a torrent that was soon to ebb as other interests took its place, including that of the new 'autocars'.

A young man of Martin's physical prowess would no doubt have welcomed the challenges and the freedoms that cycling offered. He himself records that he obtained his first machine, a Singer, as a reward for having held up his mother as she attempted to master the intricacies of balance demanded of a novice lady cyclist. He goes on to record that soon after being given his first bike he joined a 'crammers' at which a number of similar young men were keen cyclists. Martin remarks that he and they used to set out to scour the country on their cycles, their most frequent route taking them to Chipping Norton, with many a 'scrap' en route.

The Singer was changed for a newer pattern racing Osmond, but that 'scrapping' had not entirely driven out 'cramming' was evidenced by Martin's successful entry to the University of Oxford, where he became an undergraduate at Marcon's Hall, a small private Hall registered by the University, of which there were two or three in Oxford at the time. Marcon's Hall (named after the Master) only ran to two lecturers in addition to the Master himself, and some twenty or so undergraduates.

Among the delights and privileges that membership of the University offered, the use of a cinder track for cycle (path) racing stood high in Martin's estimation, and he himself recorded in later years that it was here, with his racing Osmond, that he caught the speed bug that never really left him all his life. By September 1899 he was making the headlines, locally at any rate, for his achievements on the track. By 1900 he was representing the University and had become a member of that illustrious body, the Oxford University Bicycle Club, known by the initials O.U.Bi.C. to distinguish it from the older and even more exclusive O.U.B.C. whose members disported themselves on the water. In that same year *The Sportsman* wrote: 'In L.W.B. Martin and H.B. Fitzherbert, Oxford possesses two of the best cyclists they have had for some time', a comment perhaps prompted by Martin's 2nd and two 3rd places for Oxford University in the 1-, 4- and 10-mile events respectively against United Hospitals. In the same year, riding against Cambridge, he brought home an Oxford win, plus a 2nd and a 4th place and also won the Amateur Cycling Association's Championship 10-mile event, with Curtis-Bennett (later Sir Henry, K.C.) in second place. By this time Martin had become a member of the Amateur Cycling Association and of the Anerley Bicycle Club.

W.R. Morris who, it must be remembered, made his mark in cycle racing for Oxford long before he became, as Lord Nuffield, one of its better-known benefactors, beat Martin very narrowly in the 1- and 10-mile Championships of the Berks, Oxon and South Bucks centre of the ACA in 1900, Martin being but a foot behind Morris at the end of the ten-mile event! The following year Martin could not better third place for Oxford University against United Hospitals, but when pitted against the rival University of Cambridge he romped home in first place for Oxford in all three of the 10-miles-and-under events, and secured another win in the same Centre's mile championship held at Palmer Park, Reading. In 1900 and 1901 he rode in many open events with some success, and he and Curtis-Bennett took the ¾-mile unpaced tandem record from a standing start.

In January, 1902, by which time his private address was given as 7, St Leonard's Mansions, St Leonard's Terrace, Chiswick, West London, he joined the Bath Road Club, a club which enjoyed a very high reputation among speed men of the time and of which a cycling journal, *The Hub*, had written in September 1896: "The Bath Road Cycling Club is probably the most 'toney' and select of all the road clubs, its muster-roll being rigorously limited to 130. The Marquis of Queensberry and Sir John Aird, M.P., are, amongst others, active members: and at the present time more than one representative of the aristocracy awaits the opening of a vacancy in its coveted ranks". *The Hub's* comment, unless qualified, perhaps conveys a false impression of a 'stuffy' club in which social status and snobbery outweighed enthusiasm and actual performance, but it must be remembered that in 1896 at the height of 'Society's' flirtation with cycling, such comment in the cycling press served only to emphasise that cycling had thus at last achieved a degree of social acceptance hitherto largely denied to it. As will be seen, the Bath Roaders were no snobs and 'stuffiness' was total anathema to them.

Martin had been proposed as a member of the Bath Road by T.H.B. Vade-Walpole who was not to regret his sponsorship of the new member. Indeed, Martin soon made a very favourable impression on his clubmates and a month after his acceptance the Club's magazine records, "Martin, our new member, would seem to be very hot stuff, he means to be one of the early worms and rides down the Ripley road nearly every day, making roadwork the basis of his preparation for the track...." It was not only his degree of physical fitness ("What must it feel like to be so 'orrid fit?" bemoans a fellow Bath Roader, of Martin) but his capacity for enjoying himself that impressed. "As Martin feasted it was a treat to see fat James gazing at him in open-mouthed astonishment, not unmixed with envy...." and "Really, this chap Martin *is* hot stuff; we, who used to rather fancy ourselves, could only gaze at him astonished. Besides being a fine trencherman, he would seem to be a very fair draughtsman — two tankards of old ale seemed to come not at all amiss to him...." were typical comments.

By May 1902 the Club records, "Martin, the man of girth and old ale, was up in front to make the pace...." and make the pace he did, often leaving the fastest of his companions panting in his wake. In that month he represented the Club in the famous Anfield "100", his first race for the Bath Road, and it was the general opinion that he would do well. Alas, the

15

dreaded puncture intervened and made nonsense of such predictions, and as ill-luck would have it the same misfortune was to befall him in several more Club events, so that it was not until July of 1902 that his personal fortunes turned. He set a splendid example in his regular attendance at Club runs and as always, took disappointments such as his run of tyre troubles philosophically. Certainly he allowed such misfortunes to cause him no lack of sleep or appetite, and the Bath Roaders record of him on their Henley run that the "chief incident of a good dinner was Martin's wonderful form. He continued going very well within himself long after everyone else had finished."

In July of that year he successfully completed a Bath Road 50-mile event in 2 hours 31 minutes 8 seconds — "no mean performance" as a fellow member recorded, adding, "Well done, Martin."....especially so when one recalls the state of the roads at that time. Another side of Martin's character was blossoming, his willingness and ability to get the best out of others, for his proposer of less than a year earlier, Vade-Walpole (known in the Club as "Tadpole"), put up a splendid performance in two Club events that summer, earning for Martin the comment "....some credit is due to Martin for the way in which he has brought the Tadpole out. Truly, it might be said that the Tadpole was trained, entered and ridden by Martin".

If Martin impressed his fellow Bath Roaders it is certain too that they impressed him, above all, perhaps, by their tremendous enthusiasm and sheer sense of 'joie-de-vivre' and a friendly sense of humour of a kind that often took the form of 'skylarking' and practical jokes. The Club was out and Martin with them virtually every week-end and in this way Martin amassed an encyclopaedic knowledge of most of the roads of the Home Counties and an equally astute knowledge of the inns and their old ale.

In August of that year he and Vade-Walpole joined forces in an expedition by tandem to Scotland and back — "training spins" as Martin termed the whole exercise — during which they covered some 1200 miles and wore out four pairs of tyres and had a hair-raising escape when their only brake collapsed while they were descending one of the steepest hills. All this excitement was, however, but an overture to one of Martin's finest cycling performances carried out in August 1902, when the many rumours that were flying both inside and outside the Bath Road Club that Martin was itching to attempt the Land's-End to London record were borne out. At 7.06 a.m. on Wednesday 27 August he set out from that well-known hostelry at Land's-End to make the attempt.

16

In less than a mile from the start Martin had skidded in the dust and fallen, slightly bending a pedal pin, but he remounted and rode so strongly that his supporters had great difficulty in keeping him in sight. At Bodmin, where he arrived 34 minutes ahead of schedule, news of his record attempt had leaked out and a large crowd had assembled to watch his passing. Pressing on strongly he reached Exeter over fifty minutes ahead of schedule and a halt for refreshments was made. *The Bath Road News* records that during the record run Martin's staple food was "fowl, tons of chicken legs, washed down with quarts, we may safely say gallons, of ginger ale and milk!" (Ginger ale and milk were much favoured by some long-distance riders at this period.)

By Taunton he was over an hour inside his scheduled time, so early that the food laid on him for him had not apeared and the hastily improvised arrangements caused some delay. Martin, however, discovered somewhere a plate of greengages and wolfed the lot. By Devizes night had set in, a very dark and somewhat foggy night, and Martin, hardly able to see, had perforce to slacken his pace. Dawn brought an improvement in the weather and visibility and he picked up again, so that by Theale he was once more an hour and ten minutes ahead of schedule. On through Reading and Maidenhead he kept up a cracking pace, but by Slough the road conditions were much worse and compelled him to ease off once more. Nearer still to London the tramlines were wet and greasy and the greatest care was needed in negotiating them. Full of spirit to the last, Martin even sprinted from Hammersmith, to arrive comparatively fresh at Hyde Park Corner at 05·22·16 on the Thursday morning, having knocked 3 hours 9 minutes and 16 seconds off the previous record. He rode a free-wheel Rover geared to 69 for the run, the machine being fitted with brakes. (Despite the obvious dangers which the NCU and CTC had repeatedly pointed out, many record attempts were made by brakeless machines in the early days of pneumatic safeties, but by 1902 this foolhardy practice was dying out.) For once, Martin's ride was totally devoid of the puncture bogey, though he was at one period troubled by the need to re-inflate his back tyre repeatedly.

With this record in his pocket, a record which reflected great credit on the Bath Road Club and added greatly to Martin's personal repute, one might be forgiven for thinking that Martin would ease off for a while. But not he, for in the autumn of that year he was out on all the Club runs and also assisted the fellow club members and riders from other clubs in their long-distance rides. He still delighted to quaff large quantities of old ale, to the extent that a fellow Bath Roader commented, "When we sat down to dinner Martin, as usual, began to whine for old ale. We knew he wouldn't

17

be happy until he got it, so enquiry was made as to the insidious gargle. They had some old ale on draught which was said to be 17 years old. Perhaps!, but it certainly was good!''

Subconsciously perhaps, but equally insidiously, the spell of the motor was insinuating itself into Martin's life, brought about in part, perhaps, by the following incident. When returning from a Club run to Maidenhead, Martin and a fellow rider were passed by a motor and they decided to give chase and sprinted after it. Martin's fellow rider soon fell back but Martin hung on and tucked in behind it, using the car as a pacemaker, but when passing through Slough he skidded and fell. Much shaken and with torn and tattered clothes but fortunately no broken bones, Martin was 'patched up' at ''The Crown'' while a repairer was called in to straighten the bent cycle. Shortly after this episode Martin bought a 2¾hp chain-drive Humber motor-cycle, a successful design using Phelon & Moore patents.

At the Bath Road Dinner in December 1902 Martin received an ovation as he went to collect the gold record-breaker's button and a special prize awarded by the Club, and to add to the success of the occasion he was also able to announce his B.A. degree; quite a year! Amidst the hilarity some gloom was cast by the fact that Martin and an old friend had parted company, the old friend in question being the long and elegant moustache that Martin had sported during his undergraduate days. Now it was gone and was evidently missed by others than Martin himself. Perhaps it signified the successful end to his days as undergraduate! In later years, of course, those who knew Martin would have been amazed and amused at the notion of the hefty moustache sported by the young undergraduate, but at the time a fellow Bath Roader was known to have commented, ''.....first, we must confess, we didn't know Martin. Our Land's-Ender had shaved off his lovely moustache, and it *did* make a difference. Martin *was* quite a nice-looking chap, but without his moustache — well — we will only say he looked much better *with* it.....''

From the time the new Humber motor-cycle was acquired the lure of motor-powered speed was to become more and more important in Martin's life, yet he remained intensely loyal to his cycling interests, not without interruptions it is true, but it seemed that always his deepest needs for satisfaction could only come through his own unassisted exertions. It should not be thought, however, that Martin was alone among Bath Roaders in his enthusiasm for the motor, for even among such a dedicated bunch of cycling enthusiasts there were quite a number who took an early interest in the motoring world. Montagu S. Napier, for example, was a Bath Roader who, particularly after

18

his association with the dynamic S.F. Edge, ex-racing cyclist turned racing motorist, was already by this date (1903) famous as the progenitor of England's leading racing cars, the Napiers. Writing many years later Martin recalled his first sight of a motor car in motion. "How well I remember my first sight of a motor car in motion! I was cycling from my crammers to London along the Oxford road when I saw the monster approaching and I threw myself and 'iron' into the nearest ditch, counting myself lucky to escape with my life....."

1903 brought more kudos to Martin, for he was elected Captain of the Bath Road Club, in itself remarkable for one who had been a member for only a year. This brought many additional responsibilities and, typically, Martin took his new-found tasks seriously. In January 1903 is recorded, "Lionel Martin's methods of training are varied and peculiar. His latest idea is to drag a trailer about with a lady on board. What a dog it is! And down Acre Road, too, so as to avoid meeting anyone on Surbiton Parade. Well, well! Now we know what makes him so strong.....", while on a more serious note (if one reads between the lines) his methods of ensuring that there was a good turnout for Club runs during his Captaincy drew forth the comment in March, 1903, ".....All the week Martin goes about beating up members with a woe-begone face (Martin's, not the members!), promises them their pet gargle if they will turn up and if they won't he goes home and prepares postcards with maps of the route.....These then go to the recalcitrant members. Result.....a crowd of anything from a dozen members *and* two motor-cycles. If you don't quite understand, remember that Martin 'collects' the money from these crowds after dinner. He is an awfully nice chap and a jolly captain, so what more can we want?" As for the motor-cycles, I quote a comment from the same source in May 1903, "Really, the way motor bicycles are used in the Club at the present time is little short of scandalous. Here's our Captain, Leonard — beg pardon, Lionel, of Lionel Mansions, turning up on a club run and being an hour late for lunch!"

In the Club's '25' of May, 1903, Martin put up fastest time of 1h.12m.33s., a time that had only twice been bettered previously in Bath Road '25s'. Only a short while before this performance he had joined his old tandem colleague Vade-Walpole in another tandem trip to Scotland at Easter. Easter fell early that year but despite this Martin and Vade-Walpole decided to attempt to beat the RRA Edinburgh — York record. The pundits all said it was much too early in the season to attempt such a record on that route, foretelling bad road conditions and even worse weather possibilities. Nothing, however, could daunt the two Bath Roaders and they set forth from the GPO in

19

Edinburgh at 7.0am on the Saturday morning. All too soon the forebodings of the pundits came true, for as the riders moved southwards over the hills they first came up against a wickedly strong headwind, then sleet and snow showers. Worse was to come, for before reaching Newcastle they encountered roads so deeply rutted in snow that they had to walk for three miles *downhill*. Luckily the wind veered for a time and with the wind now astern of them they lowered their heads and made good time and some fast work was put in. A ten-minute halt for food and then the prospect of an 80-mile grind against the wind, for it had changed direction yet again. The prospect of success seemed to fade but after another halt for food at Northallerton the weather temporarily eased and despite the last few miles into York being accomplished in pouring rain they reached York GPO at 7.17pm, having beaten the RRA standard by 43 minutes.

In August 1903 Martin was on holiday at Eastbourne, and the latter part of his first year's captaincy of the Bath Road was marred by a very severe attack of lumbago which for a time kept him confined to his home and left him with little prospect of resuming active cycling until Christmas. Commenting on this *The Bath Road News* remarks, "Martin has indeed had most adverse conditions to contend with, and it is greatly to his credit that the club has been so active this year". However, he was about again at Christmas and was re-elected Captain of the club for 1904, though in fact he relinquished this office at the end of October of that year. Writing many years later and recalling the first year of Martin's captaincy, J. Cecil Paget recalls, "I remember Cranford Hall in 1903, HQ of the Bath Road Club, where hospitality was lavished on guests to such an extent that a North Road writer remarked that the Bath Road men, captained by Martin, were overwhelming with attention and kindness and left nothing undone to ensure comfort and enjoyment. We even found our shoes in the morning growing on a large tree in the garden!" A comment, this, that is revealing of Martin's character. For him, indeed, nothing was too much trouble and he would go to endless pains to help others, yet his sense of fun and love of practical joking were never far below the surface.

Late in 1903, when he had recovered from his lumbago, he took to a brand-new racing tricycle, a type of machine that was to play a significant part in his future cycling activities. However, about this time he took a step further towards his motoring ambitions, for he joined forces with an old cycling friend, the latter well-known to S.F. Edge, who had the sole concession for De Dion and Napier cars for Surrey and Sussex. One cannot help feeling that fellow Bath Roader Montagu Napier may himself have had a hand in this development; indeed, he may well have been the instigator of it.

1. Vaughan's House, Eton College, July
1896. Lionel Martin is 4th from the right in the
first standing row

2. The Race Track at Palmer's Park, Reading, where some of Lionel Martin's earliest cycling successes took place

4. A page from the Bath Road archives

NAME	ELECTED	MEMBERSHIP CEASED
Martin, L. W. B.	Jan. 7. 1902	Killed on his bicycle by a motor car 21/10/45 age 67.

OFFICE HELD AND PERIOD.	NOTABLE RIDES ETC.
Captain - 1903, and Jan. to Oct. 1904. Committee - Nov. 1904 to Jan. 1905. Nov. 1909 - 1910. 1911. 1912. 1913. 1914. 1915. 1916 . 1917 R.R.A. Delegate : 1904, 10,11, 13, 1913 . 1914. 1915, 1942, 1944, 1945. Vice President : 1920. 21, 1922, 1923, 1924, 1925, 1926, 1927, 1928, 1929, 1930. 1931. 1932. 1933. 1934, 1935, 1936. 1937, 1938 1939, 1940 . 1941, 1942, 1943, 1944, 1945. Address :— Palings, Warboys Road, Kingston Hill Mongewell Cottage Pembroke Villas Holyport, Berks.)	R.R.A. records :— 1902 Land's End - London safety bicycle. 1903 Edinburgh - York tandem safety. 1911 Edinburgh - York tricycle. Gave the National "Horwood Trophy" to R.T.T.C. Martin was knocked down by a car on the 14th suffering a relapse died on Sunday Oct 21st 1945 in Kingston City Hospital

LIBRARY BUREAU LTD.   L72618

3. Martin's candidature for election as a member of the Bath Road Club, 1902

CANDIDATE FOR ELECTION.

Candidate's full Christian and Surnames ... ...) *Lionel Walker Birch Martin*

Of what other Clubs a Member...) *Oxford University Bicycle Club. Amateur Cycling Association, Anerley Bicycle Club.*

Private Address *7. St Leonard's Mansions*

St Leonard's Terrace. Chelsea S.W.

Business Address (if any) ... ...)

Occupation or Profession ...) *Undergraduate*

Have you competed in any races? If so, state your fastest time for 25, 50, and 100 miles, and when and where ridden ...) *have never competed on the Road.*

(nor on the track over 10 miles)

Candidate's Signature *Lionel Martin*

Proposed by *T.H.B. Vade-Walpole*) Who vouch for
the correctness of
Seconded by *J Burden Barnes*) the above particulars.

This form to be returned to the Hon. Sec., J. BURDEN BARNES, 18, Victoria Street, Westminster, S.W.

[P.T.O.

CYCLING SPORT
on Road and Track
in 1911.

THE ROAD : A Resume of the Year.

By "ROBIN HOOD."

N looking back on the year's road sport, one's first impression is that the fixture list is steadily becoming overcrowded. It is not easy to point to any particular racing event and say that it is superfluous, and there has not been any serious clashing of dates, but two forms of sport seem to be undergoing the painful process of being squeezed out altogether. It is almost certain that the great slump in hill-climbing is due to the increasingly heavy programme of road races, and the noticeable decline of interest in record breaking may also be traced in a considerable measure to the same cause, although it is obvious that the stiffening of record figures makes men grow more and more chary of attacking them.

It is not usual to open the road-racing season so early as Easter, but this year the Etna C.C., a progressive young club, tried the experiment of holding an open "50" on Good Friday, and a f..ly representative " field " was secured. F. H. Grubb, who had earlier been scheduled for an attempt on Green's 50 miles record, and was therefore expected to be in ripe form, was on scratch, but punctured, and fastest time honours went to L. C. Palmer, of the North London C.C., who, by doing 2 hrs. 29 min. 28 sec., just managed to beat P. C. Gibbs, Spencer C.C., by four seconds. The handicap, naturally a lottery so early in the year, was secured by M. G. Selbach, a member of the Old Crescent Wheelers, whose time of 2 hrs. 33 min. 21 sec. was much too good for a 17 min. allowance.

Next on the list was the North London "50," decided on 20th May. For the first time C. Moss appea ' as a competitor in thi. vent, sharing the scratch mark with F. H. Grubb. The latter, however, was off colour and retired, leaving Moss to

carry off the honours with a splendid ride of 2 hrs. 23 min. 1 sec. H. H. Gayler, Polytechnic C.C., was successful in the handicap, doing 2 hrs. 30 min. 11 sec., with an allowance of 11 min. The team race, a subsidiary but interesting feature, found the Polytechnic C.C. victorious, with an average of 2 hrs. 30 min. 27 sec.

On Whit Monday two important events were decided, namely the Anfield and Beaumont "100's." In the former C. Moss, Midland C. and A.C., again registered a fastest, beating record for the course by doing 5 hrs. 11 min. 52 sec. F. H. Grubb retired, owing to a puncture, when holding the leading position at approximately three-quarter distance. First handicap place fell to J. W. Kirk, a young member of the Yorkshire Road

L. W. B. Martin, Bath Road Club, holder of the Edinburgh-York tricycle record.

Club, who proved to be the " discovery " of the year, for he subsequently placed a number of fine rides to his credit. On this occasion, in spite of a puncture, he did 5 hrs. 26 min. 35 sec., with an allowance of 33 min. The other placed riders were W. R. Lempriere, North Road C.C., and H. H. Gayler, Polytechnic C.C. In the Beaumont "100," H. G. Cook, of the University C.C., put up a brilliant ride of 5 hrs. 0 min. 27 sec., securing first place in the handicap from virtual scratch. By taking the fastest time award he was debarred from participation in the handicap prizes, however, and the first was awarded to A. J. Stokes, Arab C.C., whose actual time was 5 hrs. 15 min. 49 sec.

Another new event figured on the card in Whit-week, this being the Kingsdale "50," decided on 10th June. A good out-and-home course was found north of London, and an excellent race resulted, notwithstanding that it so quickly followed the Whit-Monday competitions. Fastest time was registered by W. J. Webb, of the North Road C.C., whose club also won the team race. This was Webb's first success in open events, and his time of 2 hrs. 23 min. 29 sec. represented first-class travelling. H. Smith, of the Unity C.C., was successful in the handicap from the limit mark of 15 min., his time being 2 hrs. 31 min. 25 sec. The Kingsdalers were fortunate in their weather, but the same cannot be said of the Manchester Wheelers, who entered the field a fortnight later with an open "50" in Shropshire. Rain fell in torrents, and it speaks well for the pertinacity of the riders that so many completed the course in creditable time. C. Moss punctured, and D. R. Noon, of the Speedwell, who only decided to start at the last moment, ran out with fastest time, namely 2 hrs. 32 min. 19 sec.—a fine performance for such a day. The handicap went to another prominent Birmingham rider in the person of

1

5. Lionel Martin after his Edinburgh - York tricycle record, 1911

6. The motorist woos the cyclist; an advertisement that appeared in *The Bath Road News,* 1914

7. Lionel Martin in the specially tuned Singer with which he had so many competition successes

8. Lionel Martin's grey Silver Ghost Rolls-Royce saloon

9. The original? Martin at the wheel of AM4656, known in the Works as 'Coal Scuttle'

10. Complete with the celebrated poncho and 'gor blimey' cap, Lionel Martin surveys AM270 in one of its very early forms

11. Katherine Martin at the wheel of 'Coal Scuttle' at Brooklands, 1921

12. Katherine Martin in close-up, at the wheel of the same car

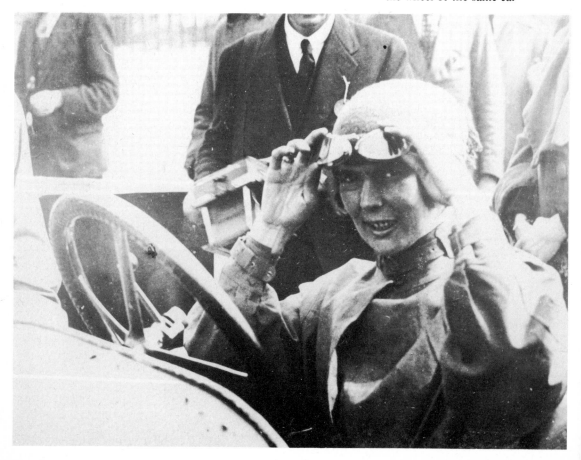

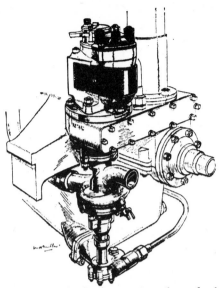

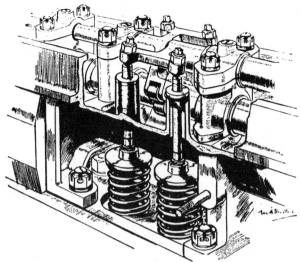

Spigot mounting for the magneto on the overhead valve Aston-Martin. The shaft which drives the magneto drives also the water and oil pumps.

Sketch showing the interlaced rocking levers on the overhead valve Aston-Martin engine. Each lever terminates in a fork which operates a tappet.

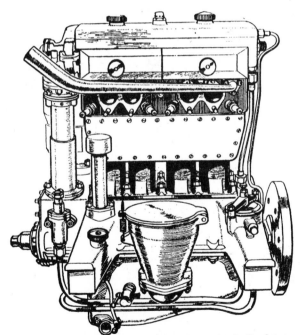

Four overhead valves are used for the engine in the Aston-Martin racer to be driven by Count Zborowski. The valves have an overhead camshaft. On the side of the crank case is an enormous funnel through which oil can be introduced to the sump.

13, 14 & 15.   Three drawings of the Robb single-ohc engine, 1921

16. 'Calamity' Kate gets her artistic talents to work in the Paddock

17. A youthful 'Bertie' Kensington Moir, Lionel Martin and Robert Bamford pose behind a later version of AM270. Note the unusual side-mounted spare wheel, more often carried astern on this car

18.   Lionel and Katherine Martin in AM270 in a Land's
-End Trial

19.   Lionel Martin with B.S.
Marshall and his mechanic
Papworth with 'Bunny' at Le
Mans for the GP des Voitur-
ettes, September 1921

20. Clive Gallop poses in 'Bunny', seen here carrying the long tailed track body

21. Proving trip to the Isle of Man prior to the 1922 TT: Lionel Martin, Kensington Moir, Clive Gallop and Count 'Lou' Zborowski pose in Ramsey behind the snow-covered Aston

22. Kensington Moir takes 'Bunny' round Windy Corner in the 1922 "1500 Trophy" as part of the TT. The writing "Rabbit at Windy Corner, 3900 on bottom gear" is in Kate's hand

23. 'Bunny' during the famous World's Record bid at Brooklands, May 1922. Gallop attends to the off-side front wheel, 'Sammy' Davis (in overalls) looks at the engine, beside him stands Katherine Martin. Lionel busies himself with refuelling watched by the Shell representative and Jack Addis is busy investigating the cockpit

24. Another close-up of the record bid: Clive Gallop is in the cockpit and beside the car are Kensington Moir (in white sweater) and 'Sammy' Davis (in overalls)

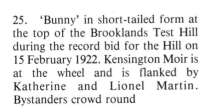

25. 'Bunny' in short-tailed form at the top of the Brooklands Test Hill during the record bid for the Hill on 15 February 1922. Kensington Moir is at the wheel and is flanked by Katherine and Lionel Martin. Bystanders crowd round

26. Strasbourg, 1922. Kensington Moir at the wheel of Zborowski's car, the latter's mechanic beside him. In the background 'Queenie', the Ford-T van used as the Works' hack and nicknamed by Mrs Martin

27.   C.G. Stead in 'Bunny' on the occasion of the 200-Miles Race, 1922, when he so nobly upheld the honour of the make by finishing second to K. Lee Guinness in the Talbot-Darracq and just pipping Segrave's similar car in third place. An amazing performance!

28.   Eddy Hall disports himself with 'Bunny' at Aston Clinton and is seen here controlling a slide

29. Eddy Hall in 'Bunny',
unusually with road equipment
photographed early in 1924

30. How beautifully 'Bunny' captures the essence of the early 1920's speed hill-climb in this shot, with Moir at the wheel

31. One would need a close look to distinguish 'Bunny' in retirement here, pictured when in the ownership of Dallas Brett

32. Lionel Martin with AM270 at
Brooklands, passing a Horstman

33. Zborowski in the single ohc Robb-engined car at Brooklands in June 1922. Lionel Martin stands on the left
and Jack Addis astern. The depression seen on the tail immediately beneath Addis's tie is the "bloody great kink"
put there by F.G. Hunt when riding on the tail to the start of the race!

CHAPTER TWO

Early in 1905 Martin wrote to his Bath Road colleagues from Nice where he had spent much of the winter of 1904, and he reported that he had looked in on the great motor and cycle exhibition in Paris. He comments on the standard of French machines (at the same time regretting the paucity of English ones, mentioning only the Humbers and the Pedersens). Whereas he found many of the French cycles attractive, he bemoaned the fact that on the whole France was not good cycling country, particularly castigating the abundance of pavé and tramlines. He remarked too on the few cyclists encountered on the open road and the number met with in towns; "poor chaps, the trams and motors must make life unbearable for them," he concludes. He confesses to having a car in France, a 24-32hp Mors which he describes as "quite a sporting turnout; it will do just over 50mph." He speaks glowingly of a friend's 60hp Mercedes and remarks that he hopes to drive home across France, some 760 miles. "I have seen three Napiers here," he adds.....perhaps a reflection of his British interests in the motoring field at this period. Martin was to remain a friend of Montagu Napier until the latter's death in 1931.

Martin's increasing interest in motoring, coupled, alas, with bouts of ill-health, took him away from the active cycling scene over the next few years. He had been a member of the Bath Road committee from November 1904 to January 1905 and an RRA Delegate in 1904, but he then did not serve on the Bath Road committee until November 1909 and he was re-appointed an RRA Delegate in 1910. However, during the 1905 to 1910 period he was more and more immersed in the motoring scene, demonstrating Napiers and De Dions up and down the country, and incidentally acquiring a wide experience of many different makes of motor car. A period which he himself described as "a very profitable partnership".

A fellow Bath Roader recorded in September 1905, ".....it was pleasing to get a glimpse of Martin once more. He was disporting himself on the river near Windsor one recent Sunday and looked as cheery and happy as ever.

And so fat!", a comment amplified two months later by "Martin has grown quite fat and has such a lovely double chin. He gets about a bit in his motor, but is afraid to take cycle exercise at present".....this, presumably, a reference to his recurrent bouts of ill-health.

In 1907 Martin moved to 21 Grove Court, Drayton Gardens, London SW, and in June of that year a Bath Roader commented, "Martin flashed by in his car, but his spark was too far advanced to enable him to stop.....", this on the occasion of the Bath Road Club's Photo Run to Cobham. One detects a nostalgic note in a comment of November that year that "L.M. has taken to a push bike again.....Ah-h-h-h-h-h!", a remark echoed by a further comment of January 1908 which read, ".....who knows but that he will be coming out on a bicycle, and show us how they quaffed old ale in days of yore".

In 1909 unforeseen factors edged Martin back into the active cycling fold once again. His love of speed brought him into minor conflict with authority and in July the Richmond justices fined him £20 with 9 guineas costs and the Guildford Bench mulcted him of a further fine of £10 with £6.10s.6d. costs, apparently for his refusal to attend on summons to be identified for previous "fast little bits on the road", as *The Bath Road News* reported. In November the same source reported further, "Here is a warning to our motoring members; Lionel Martin, we hear, has taken to cycling again, having had his driving licence suspended for two or three years, but he is getting his fat off.....". (Happily, his suspension was for the shorter period as he was motoring again in May 1911).

In October (1909) *The Bath Road News* reported, "We were all glad to welcome Lionel Martin out on club runs once more." By November of that year he was re-elected to the Club's committee on which he was to continue to serve without a break until 1917. He was also appointed RRA Delegate in 1910, continuing in this capacity until 1915.

By the end of the year (1909) Martin was evidently resigned to his enforced spell of no driving, having lost his appeal against the forfeiture of his licence, which drew forth the comment in *The Bath Road News*, "Lionel Martin has lost his appeal against the 'peelers'. Shall we say we are sorry or glad — the latter, we think, from the Club's point of view." And indeed, the next few years were to prove significant in Martin's active participation in cycling, and perhaps more significant than he could have imagined in influencing future events. Certainly things were to take a different turn from what he might have expected when first faced with an unwelcome driving ban.

The Bath Roaders were pleased indeed to see their old captain back with them again. In January 1910, on the club's run to Godstone, a fellow member recorded, "the chief item of interest during lunch was Sir Lion Hell's cross-examination of mine host on the subject of old ale. Many searching enquiries did he put as to the age, origin, taste, smell, colour, strength and specific gravity of the 'Clayton Arms' stock, and the replies being satisfactory, ordered a beaker, which he proceeded to quaff with great gusto. "Though swallows twain do not a summer make, yet one good swallow and a Martin take the cake for old ale shifting.....!" In the Bath Road "50" in May Martin put up the fastest time of 2h.32m.44s., ample evidence that he had lost none of his old skill.

In the period between Martin's active cycle racing with the Bath Road and his return to the fold following his brush with the justices, one Robert Bamford had joined the Bath Road. Bamford, son of The Revd R. Bamford M.A. (Cantab), was apprenticed to Messrs Hesse & Savory at their Teddington Launch Works and was set on an engineering career. Although he never achieved cycling feats comparable to those of Martin he was nevertheless a very keen and active club member, popular with his fellows and a fast and stylish rider. Lionel Martin, on his return to activity with his old club, came to recognise in Bamford something of a kindred spirit.

Lionel Martin had first been seen mounted on a racing tricycle as early as 1903 and it was largely on three-wheelers that his future Club successes were gained. In August 1910 he put up a distance of 301¾ miles in 24 hours on such a machine, a Club record that stood for some thirty years. However, he still suffered from intermittent bouts of ill-health, but in May 1911 he regained his driving licence after the ban that had been imposed on him, and at this time he was reported as having been seen by members of the Bath Road on Easter Monday, ".....driving a 100hp car, tearing up the nice country roads and spoiling them for nice, quiet, unoffending cyclists....." One can hardly be surprised that he would be delighted to get back behind the wheel of a fast car again after an enforced absence from such pleasures, but for all that, 1911 was a year in which his tricycle performances were to be notable indeed.

Perhaps with a view to training for his own star performance he took part in the Land's-End to London event, and as so often in years past, was invaluable in his help to competitors and organisers alike, it being reported of him that "he was carrying a capacious bag on the back of his machine, with a spare gas lamp, two bottles of drink, grapes, and, in fact, a travelling William Whiteleys". He had earlier taken part in the Bath and

43

Back Ride on a fixed-wheel tricycle pulling a gear of 65, when he was reported to be suffering from lack of sleep through turning out to help in record attempts, but as usual, he rode splendidly and gave the utmost assistance to the whole party.

All this activity was leading up to his own performance of October, 1911, when he established a new Edinburgh-York tricycle record, setting up a new time of 13 hours 54 minutes. This was no mean achievement for a man of 33, especially when one considers his recent bouts of illness and resultant absence from active cycling. Martin left the GPO at Edinburgh at 7.30am on Friday, 13 October (no victim of superstition, he) after what a contemporary describes as "a ponderous breakfast". Despite a puncture shortly after the start, he reached Coldstream seven minutes ahead of schedule, where, as the same contemporary puts it, "a collation was in readiness and ample justice was done to the succulent fare." Martin's stamina over the hilly route near Bridge of Alan drew forth much favourable comment and the apparently indefatigable rider pedalled on southwards, through Durham to Darlington, which he reached at 5·47pm. Another meal was eaten ("with gusto", I quote) and a lamp was attached to the tricycle's lamp-bracket. By now the faint mists that he had met near Durham had thickened to icy cold swirling wreaths of fog, but his pace never slackened and he reached the GPO at York triumphantly at 9·24pm, having beaten the former record held by Dr F.W. Wesley of the North Road CC by 33 minutes. An enthusiastic crowd welcomed and cheered him and he then retired to the Adelphi Hotel.

The Bath Road News reported the record run in the following month's issue commenting, "It is a matter of great congratulation to the club that Martin should have succeeded in again attacking a record after so many years abstention from the sport." In the same issue another writer remarked, "We have not seen Martin for about seven years. He looked horribly fit, which seems a good advertisement for the push variety of velocipede." The leading periodical for the pastime, *Cycling*, carried a good photograph of Martin on his record-breaking machine, the caption remarking "His return to the field of record-breaking — after a lapse of motoring — is exceedingly welcome." Note the use of the word "lapse"! Incidentally, this record of Martin's stood for fifteen years.

The following year, 1912, saw Martin out with the Bath Roaders on many occasions. Often Robert Bamford was out with him, both men as often as not in the van of the riders, for Martin always liked to make the pace. The following quotation from the club journal well illustrates this: "Well, you chaps," said Martin, "I don't feel much like keeping up a horrid speed all

44

the way back, so I'll just go on slowly", and off he went. Less than two minutes after, everyone was in full pursuit, intending to dash past him with fiendish yells of diabolical mockery. Early in the chase Webb, who led, was rewarded by a glimpse of Martin going slowly along at about the speed of the winner of the Waterloo Cup all out. Pound away as hard as he could, Old Buck had not an earthly chance of catching the elusive one, who finally faded (no doubt smiling) away into the twilight and was seen no more....."

That summer Martin was present with many other Bath Roaders at an old-established and favourite event, the Anfield "100", usually held in the Shrewsbury area. The Bath Roaders would make their way there by various means, some riding the whole way from London, others travelling by train, their machines in the luggage van, and by this time (1912), some by motor-car. The Club made it a regular practice to put up at "The Bath Arms" at Minsterley, a village some eleven miles south-west of Shrewsbury, set in delightful countryside. It is to that pleasant spot that the following quotation refers. "All Sunday we 'lopped abaht' in the garden till the arrival of Martin, the mechanic, who was roundly abused for not coming earlier. However, when he started he speedily made good. Out came dud wheels, in went new ones, oil squirted into hubs, brackets and steering heads, and in a marvellously short space of time he, whilst we had tea on the lawn, transformed our bicycles into raging speed irons....."

Writing to me many years later, S.C.H. ('Sammy') Davis recalls, "He always took meticulous care to make certain his racing cycles were near perfect. He would spend hours until he was satisfied with the riding position, the chain adjustment and the perfection of all bearings, however small. And he always rode with a carefully thought out strategical and tactical plan." A Bath Roader of a later generation, to whom Martin had recounted some of his experiences of the period under review, recalls his description of incidents that took place when he was surveying the course prior to his Edinburgh-York tricycle record. Martin arrived at a first-class hotel near Newcastle and requested accommodation, and being clad in mud-spattered cycling clothes, he felt that his welcome was less than cordial. However, he always used to carry in his saddle-bag a lightweight uncrushable suit. He changed his clothes, sent out a request for a buttonhole flower, sailed into the hotel dining-room and ordered the best wine from the stock in the cellar. He then smiled to himself to notice the marked change in attitude of members of the hotel staff now only too ready to accord him the best possible service.

The year, and the active cycling season with it, was drawing to a close, and before its end Martin was to make a further determined step in the interests

45

of motoring. However, two further illustrations of Martin's less formal pursuits among the Bath Roaders perhaps deserve a mention in passing. Of a certain club run a member records; "..... after lunch he (Martin) was in fine form. To see him do the can-can with an uncorked bottle in each hand, without spilling any, is worth going farther than Shaftesbury to see....." After this lively lunch the party, in great good humour, took to the road again....." and springing into the saddle Li flew up the hill and out of sight in no time. But not for long. The bike had burst its back tyre on the next hairpin.....and Martin, with characteristic energy, had whipped out the front wheel and was trying to fix a spare over the tyre already there.....But in a few minutes came a roar and a rush and away flew Li up the hill and out of sight again. But not for long. Finding it impossible to overtake those in front, he conceived the idea of making a beeline across country to catch them. Jumping over a hedge and ditch, he started off across the field. But the bike had something to say to that!....."

From time to time the contributors to *The Bath Road News* deserted prosody for verse (or worse). At the risk of being accused of mangling the anonymous scribe's doggerel I quote a small part of one such outpouring of the muse:-

> 'So we sped us onwards
>   In the stilly night,
> Till, like me, exhausted,
> Out went Martin's light.
> Then from out the offing
>   Did then and there appear
> A wily nimble policeman
> To catch him by the ear.
> Was he caught? No never,
>   Turn and turn again,
> And the wily policeman
> Sought for him in vain.....'

Such simple anecdotes will find an echo in many an early cyclist's heart, no doubt.

Towards the close of the year came the news, momentous as future events were to show, that Bamford and Martin had joined forces in the running of a motor business in Callow Street, Fulham Road. This new venture drew forth the comment in the club journal that "the combined knowledge and energy of two such strenuous people should make things go, and we wish them every success in the new venture." About the time of this interesting development Martin also moved house again, settling in to 11 Sloane Square Mansions,

Sloane Square, S.W.

1913.....and indeed, new horizons.

Bamford and Martin Ltd. devoted themselves to the buying and selling and, where appropriate, to the tuning for performance, of current small cars such as the Calthorpe, G.W.K. and Singer, having secured for the latter make a sub-agency through Percy Lambert, a frequent and successful Brooklands driver who had been the first to cover over 100 miles in the hour in a 4½-litre side-valve Talbot, and who was so tragically killed at Brooklands shortly afterwards. Lionel Martin had himself purchased a 10hp Singer light car off the Olympia Show stand in 1912 and had "breathed" upon it to such good effect that this undistinguished little car of no more than average performance now could attain a rousing 70mph maximum without any sacrifice in reliability. However, the firm was not to remain long at the Callow Street address, having persuaded Hesse & Savory to allow them to take over premises at Henniker Place, South Kensington, which had formerly served as Hesse & Savory's London depot. This move from the Fulham Road brought together a third element destined to have a marked impact on later developments. This was Jack Addis, who had shortly before come from Hesse & Savory's Teddington Launch Works to take over as Works Foreman at Henniker Place, where Robert Bamford was Manager. The move also triggered off a spate of competition activity from Lionel Martin's tuned and modified Singer Ten.

The late F.G. Hunt, who was employed at Henniker Place at the time, recalls that this Singer Ten was completely stripped, the engine overhauled, and after a very extensive road testing over every type of road and under varying conditions as the tuning process developed, was given completely re-profiled cam contours for a greatly increased performance overall. Driven by Martin, often accompanied by Jack Addis, in long-distance reliability trials such as the London-Land's End or London-Exeter, many successes were gained. Over sixty years later, E.R. Cass wrote to me with his reminiscences of a London-Gloucester Trial in which he and his brother entered. On arrival at the start they found that all entrants' passengers had to be exchanged to allow each driver to be accompanied by a passenger other than his own, and Cass found himself allocated to Lionel Martin's Singer. "We had a very enjoyable run," he wrote, "but I noticed that when climbing hills Martin kept in the higher gears too long and we were soon down to first gear. On the return journey we had to climb Nailsworth Ladder, a gradient of 1-in-2½ at its steepest. As we approached the hill I advised him to change to the lowest gear and give the engine full throttle. We successfully climbed the hill but

47

burst the radiator, but concluded the run without any further trouble.''

Martin's many successes with the tuned and modified Singer led to enthusiastic requests for similar modifications to other customers' cars but Martin, already impatient at the chores and delays of constantly having to collect customers' cars from the various makers' works and the amount of time needed to carry out the modifications and tuning — to say nothing of the additional costs involved — was already formulating ideas of building his own cars to an ideal. Using an earlier Isotta-Fraschini chassis into which was fitted a new Coventry-Simplex engine of about 1400cc, the first Aston-Martin was born. When Isotta-Fraschini had introduced their 1327cc single overhead camshaft 4-cylinder engine for their small sporting model in 1908 it was much in advance of its time, and was mounted in an orthodox chassis, the whole car being finished to a very high standard of workmanship. So Lionel Martin's 1400cc prototype, registered LH 7933, saw physical existence just before world events were turned upside-down by the outbreak of war in 1914, though he did compete with it in the MCC Brighton Trial just before the wartime ban on such activities.

War, of course, brought many inevitable changes. Martin sold off all the machinery at Henniker Place to the Sopwith Aviation Co. at Kingston, Surrey, to which firm Jack Addis went as transport manager. Robert Bamford who for some years had belonged to one of the London Cyclists' Battalions joined the Army Service Corps and Lionel Martin himself worked for the Admiralty, spending some time at the Chepstow shipyards of E. Finch & Co. (1916) Ltd., which when taken over later by the Admiralty became National Shipyard No. 1 and was engaged on Admiralty contracts. The Admiralty set in train a large programme of expansion and development at Chepstow, where they brought in many thousands of shipyard workers, built an additional yard on the other side of the river at Beachley and also built three 'garden cities' for the shipyard workers and a very large hospital which later became the Ministry of Pensions Hospital. The National Shipyard turned out several War Ministry standard ships of up to 3000 tons, in addition to numerous smaller craft. Capt. George Eyston, who raced Aston-Martins in his early racing days, recalls Lionel Martin reminiscing happily about his time at Chepstow.

CHAPTER THREE

It was a vastly different world that had to face up to the very real problems of peace after the Armistice of November 1918. The survivors of those hundreds of thousands of young men who had gone to fight 'the war to end war' were lucky indeed to be survivors, luckier still if they survived without the suffering of severe physical or mental injuries that sadly afflicted so many of their numbers. The vision of Britain as a land fit for heroes may not have burned brightly in the minds of many of them but some sense of euphoria was a natural reaction to the tensions, restrictions and limited horizons of active service and the coming of peace was rapturously welcomed. To many whose mechanical awareness had been born of the stresses of war motoring in some form was a high priority on returning to civilian life, with the result that to motor manufacturers, themselves eager to return to the production of motor vehicles after years of turning out war materials of one sort or another, the stage seemed set fair for a boom period of intense demand and prosperity.

All too soon, however, shortages of materials, increasing prices, the practical difficulties of the reversion to civilian production, and labour problems were to make themselves felt in the scramble to satisfy an apparently insatiable demand from a public determined to become mobile in almost anything at almost any cost.

Lionel Martin, whose first prototype had seen the light of day only just before the outbreak of war, was, paradoxically, both better placed and at a disadvantage when compared with the established motor manufacturers. Whereas wartime demand had been reflected in a materially increased production from the mining company, Singleton Birch Ltd., from which he drew his income, he, unlike those already well established, had no proven designs ready to go into production to meet the immediate demand. That his own finances had been boosted must have been an encouraging factor to one whose ideal of a 'perfect' sporting light car remained as clear and compelling as ever but which, if it was to be brought to fruition, was bound to be a very expensive project.

He was now faced with the task of bringing to birth as a production car an ideal that, even if no setbacks were encountered, could have no more than a limited appeal to a very small number of connoisseurs. Martin as a motoring personality was still well-known and remembered by enthusiastic motorists of the pre-war era, but his Aston-Martin car was as yet little more than a gleam in its designer's eye and had yet to make any kind of a name for itself in order to attract the right kind of discerning customers; and this at a time when aspiring motor manufacturers were thick on the ground.

The first priority was to get together again the little band who had formed Bamford & Martin Ltd. before the war and at least to get a few of the new experimental cars built and tested. F.G. Hunt who, on his demobilisation from the RFC, had been told by Jack Addis not to look for another job but to return to the old firm, voluntarily forfeited his due of 28 days' demobilisation leave in order to start at once — an incident which typifies the enthusiasm and devotion to an ideal of the whole Aston-Martin project.

A move was made in January 1920 from Henniker Place to 53 Abingdon Road, Kensington, unassuming little premises next door to an United Dairies Milk Depot. The first true prototype, known as 'Coal Scuttle' and registered AM 4656 took shape and was fully described in *The Motor* in November 1919. The side-valve engine was designed by one S. Robb, lately of Coventry-Simplex, who was shortly afterwards to design a 16-valve single overhead camshaft engine as a 'hotter' alternative for the Aston-Martin, and of which more anon. With 'Coal Scuttle' in existence there began for Martin, assisted as often as not by Addis and Hunt, an intensive programme of road-testing and of competition in many of the major trials of the period which were once again resuming their place in the motor sporting calendar, just as the pre-war Isotta-Fraschini hybrid Aston had undergone some five years earlier. 'Coal Scuttle' survived this rigorous programme and in the light of experience gained Martin felt that in this form the car no longer exhibited to the full the lead in design over its contemporaries that he had set his heart on. Never one to compromise, he decided that the lessons learned must be incorporated in a modified design, though the original concept remained in essence as before. The chief modifications were the substitution of a Hele-Shaw multi-plate clutch in lieu of a cone type, a re-designed and materially lightened back-axle, a new gearbox (a splendid close-ratio box which gave a beautifully fast change) and a number of engine modifications including an increase of the stroke to 107mm, giving an overall capacity of 1486cc.

Three chassis-frames were delivered for the new design from Rubery-Owen early in 1920 but only one car, the second prototype, was in fact assembled initially from these frames. This car was fully described and illustrated in *The Autocar* of 12 March 1921. During trials of this car the chassis frame was found to be unsuitable, as Martin himself recalled in a letter many years later to (the late) F.E. Ellis: "For testing purposes three frames only were at first supplied, each designed for a wheelbase of 8′6″. These were too weak, being only 3″ deep, but we had to use them up." It was one such frame, shortened and strengthened, that formed the basis of the immortal racing Aston-Martin 'Bunny' a little later.

In all this post-war activity Lionel Martin had been joined by his second wife, Katherine. His first wife, née Christine Murray, had died shortly after the birth of their only son, John, in 1913. Katherine Martin was the vivacious, determined and at times impulsive daughter of a North Devon cleric by the name of Alexander and was one of a large and lively family. As Mrs Martin she took an intensely active and personal interest in the whole Aston-Martin project, it being entirely in her nature to throw herself whole-heartedly into whatever she undertook. She accompanied her husband on many of the proving trips with the prototype cars and indeed, revealed herself as a driver of considerable skill and accomplishment, as the following quotations from the motoring press of the time serve to show:-
"To Mrs Martin belongs the honour of being the first lady driver to pilot a car up the Ladder" (Nailsworth, near Stroud, Gloucestershire), "her machine being the Aston-Martin previously driven by her husband. She drove the car in expert fashion and put up a really good speed for the climb".....and....."Mrs Martin's remarkably daring climb is the first ever achieved by a lady under similar conditions." She was to play a vital, even if controversial rôle, in the affairs of Aston-Martin.

This intensive programme of testing by lengthy road runs and in major trials involved Martin and his enthusiastic helpers in a constant activity of preparation, planning and diagnosis and correction of minor faults. The majority of the major road trials took place at week-ends, so that on many occasions when events of this nature were taking place the week-end became merely an extension of the working week. From his early Bath Road days of competitive cycling this was, of course, a familiar pattern and Lionel always derived particular enjoyment from such activities, meticulously planning routes and mileages, comparing response and road behaviour under different conditions and carefully recording the results of such preparatory work and of modifications made. So too had he prepared his specially tuned Singer for competition before the war, and the pre-production Aston-Martins received an equally searching examination and testing.

It would be easy to assume that this uncompromising and fastidious approach to the task of putting the new cars through their paces was therefore a serious business unleavened by the sense of any than of the most limited and functional purpose. But this would be to ignore that other side of Martin's make-up which had so consistently come to the fore in his active cycle racing days — his sense of fun. As he himself wrote in *Motor Sport* in 1944 — ".....Also, we used to sally forth on the road rather in the mood of the traditional Irishman seeking someone to 'tread on the tail of his coat' and many were the hectic scraps which resulted....." and one can well imagine that though each journey might have a serious purpose in the overall plan for testing the cars no opportunity for enjoyment of other things was allowed to slip by.

Martin and his wife and young John had by this time moved closer to the Abingdon Road works of Bamford & Martin Ltd., and lived at 'The Hollies', 1 Pembroke Villas, Kensington, where a cheerfully 'open house' atmosphere prevailed and where many of the wealthy young men with motoring interests and aspirations were invited or just 'dropped in'. It was an era of peace and 'anti-war', a society to whom the new decade seemed to offer abundant promise and one in which for many pleasure-seeking assumed an almost frenetic quality in which the young and the not-so-young showed an uninhibited enjoyment of the pursuit of pleasure that was already creating the atmosphere of the 'roaring twenties'. In this well-breeched and well-connected milieu Lionel, with his charm of manner and of manners and his ever-ready sense of fun and the enjoyment of the good things of life was ably backed by Katherine who, to quote a friend with whom she later shared a number of motoring adventures, "was a wonderful housekeeper and a wonderful cook; a meal in her house was one to be remembered, plus wine from a very good cellar.....".

Lionel was an astute man and from these enjoyable and apparently casual encounters with the wealthy motoring fraternity he formed wide contacts with those who were thus drawn personally, if not deeply, into the atmosphere of the whole Aston-Martin project, and who would perhaps become favourably disposed as potential customers when the production cars became available. Not only that, but he was a shrewd judge of character as well, and was quietly assessing a number of young men whose interest in the Aston-Martin was to be more than merely that of potential customers.

It was while at 'The Hollies' that Lionel and Katherine drew into their circle the nucleus of those young motoring enthusiasts who were to play a vital part in the firm's racing fortunes, for Lionel had always realised that to sell his new products he must bring the name of Aston-Martin to the fore in competition — not just in road trials (though these carried more 'weight' in the public's estimation than was to be the case later), but in racing, and particularly at Brooklands.

Quite apart from the inevitable cost of indulging in a racing programme, Martin realised perfectly well that he must attract drivers other than himself, his wife, or Jack Addis, whose time must be increasingly taken up at the works if a racing programme, once begun, was to be kept going and the production cars were to become a reality. Perhaps Lionel's own keen sense of the value of competition as publicity and his own enjoyment of it allowed him to place undue emphasis on this aspect of the whole project, but in this attitude he was fully supported by the young men who gathered round him at this time. Their claim to be as much 'the Aston-Martin Boys' as were 'the Bentley Boys' of a few years later is, in my opinion, a valid one. Indeed, some were the self-same individuals!

To revert to mere machinery for a while. From the weakness in the frame that was revealed in the second prototype there was derived, surprisingly quickly, what may be termed a 'final' prototype with a much stiffer frame available in long (8'9") and short (8'0") wheelbase lengths. This final prototype was entirely conventional but bristled with detail features all indicative of Martin's careful attention to detail and meticulous standards. The neatly arranged adjustments provided for the pedals, the gear- and brake-levers and the rake and length of the steering-column may be taken as typical of the whole design. Another feature was the engine lubrication, the sump being of large capacity, the filtering system more than usually ample and generous by the standards of the time, and the operations of filling and draining the crankcase could be simply, quickly and cleanly carried out.

Fitted with a light aluminium cloverleaf body this 'final' prototype gave the make its first Brooklands win, appropriately enough with Lionel Martin at the wheel, at the Essex Short Handicap at Brooklands in May 1921, at a speed of 69.75mph. To the confusion of later historians Martin seems to have indulged in the frequent exchange of engines, bodies and registration numbers among the early Astons. The 'final' prototype was registered AM 270 but as this and other index numbers appeared from time to time on different cars one would be rash to assume that AM 270 is always one and the same car! However, the 'final' prototype had it first — and officially —

so for brevity I shall refer to this car as **AM 270**.

The memorably hot summer of 1921 was memorable also in the Aston-Martin camp as one of feverish activity and development. AM 270 took shape and had to be equally strenuously tested and the two remaining weak chassis frames were turned to good account. One was shortened and strengthened to become the basis of a racing car, the legendary 'Bunny'. It was Katherine who bestowed this nickname on the car and also, by the way, it was she who, having like many girls of a similar upbringing, had some artistic talent, designed the neat 'AM' monogram circular radiator badge that graced all the Bamford & Martin Astons.

Martin's Brooklands win of May 1921 was not by any means the first appearance of the new make at that venue, for among others, Jack Addis had raced an Aston there before, gaining for 'Coal Scuttle' three 2nd places and one 4th place in short events run by the JCC a year earlier. But to win is what attracts attention and the car which was to attract the greatest attention in the immediate future was 'Bunny'.

Lionel Martin had entered this car with B.S. Marshall as driver for the Grand Prix des Voiturettes at Le Mans in September 1921, a race run over the fast and difficult Le Mans circuit as a kind of junior partner to the more illustrious Grand Prix itself. Carrying the race number 4 the virtually untried Aston-Martin was pitted against formidable opposition, including a team of three new 1½-litre Talbot-Darracqs which proved to be remarkably fast and romped in to a 1-2-3 victory in the order Thomas, Guinness, Segrave. Of Marshall's performance with 'Bunny', equipped with a standard but tuned side-valve engine, Martin could scarcely fail to take pleasure. Martin, of course, had accompanied the racing team and was active in the organisation and in the pits. Marshall came home in 6th place, having made the fastest getaway of the whole field, Segrave included. By the fourth lap 'Bunny' held 4th place, but was the first car to come in to the pits, to tighten shock absorbers. By lap 8 the Aston had dropped to 7th place, but by lap 20 had moved up one position which Marshall managed to hold to the end despite a refuelling stop on the twenty-second lap. For a lone entry with a side-valve car against factory-prepared machinery of the sophistication and calibre of the Talbot-Darracqs this was a very creditable performance indeed.

It was also something of an overture, for during the year much interest and speculation had been aroused by the announcement by the Junior Car Club that they intended to hold a 200-Miles Race at Brooklands for light cars, divided into two classes, up to 1100cc and 1101 — 1500cc. The idea appealed greatly to Lionel Martin who expressed the view to the motoring press that "I think the race is the biggest thing that ever happened in the English motor world. I have entered four Aston-Martins for the race". This opinion was expressed in July 1921.

Other manufacturers were equally interested and entries poured in. Before the actual race day, October 22nd, a number had withdrawn but entries were still high and all four Aston-Martins came to the line. B.S. Marshall had 'Bunny' again, the Hon. Victor Bruce drove none other than the venerable 'Coal Scuttle' and Kensington Moir and Count 'Lou' Zborowski each had one of the new track cars, Zborowski's being that with the new single ohc 16-valve engine designed by Robb, late of Coventry-Simplex, who had also been responsible for the side-valve Aston engines. The 1½-litre Talbot-Darracqs that had gained so easy a victory at Le Mans the previous month again proved unassailable and repeated their 1-2-3-winning performance, though victory this time went to Segrave. Of the Astons, 'Bunny' with B.S. Marshall came in 9th, followed by Zborowski in the Robb ohc car, while Moir retired on the 47th lap when the fuel tank was ruptured by the back axle on one of the more notorious bumps, and Victor Bruce dropped out after taking 'Coal Scuttle' round for 61 laps.

Clearly it was time for re-appraisal. The Robb 16-valve engine, of 65mm bore × 112mm stroke, had proved a disappointment, giving but little increase of output over the tuned side-valvers, and in addition, its main bearings and its ignition arrangements were troublesome. Lionel Martin himself recalls of it in a letter to (the late) F.E. Ellis that "its incurable trouble was the centre main. It was intended to use battery ignition, and while the mounting was good enough for a light distributor head, it would not stand up to a mag. A sort of 'Heath Robinson' (with apologies to him!) rig to carry a mag. was 'designed'." The base of the Robb engine, in which the vertical magneto drive lay above the oil and water pumps driven in tandem below, was in fact perpetuated in all the later ohc Aston engines and was seldom trouble-free. Zborowski was most disappointed by its performance, for it gave only 2 or 3bhp improvement on the sv engine, and it was largely at his insistence that the design was scrapped.

With plans for the 1922 season already in the air, the winter of 1921/2 found Lionel Martin and the staff at 53 Abingdon Road up to the eyes in bringing about vital changes with a view to the 1922 season. With the inaugural Brooklands 200-Miles Race over and the potential of light car racing proven without any doubt (for the race had been won at a speed of 88·82mph and the fastest laps had both been of 93.09mph by Segrave and "K.L.G."), this seems a good opportunity to look more closely at the new personalities in the Aston camp.

'Bertie' Kensington Moir was a nephew of Sydney Straker and as a dashing young man with an irresistibly infectious laugh he had acquired some racing and sprint experience with a racing Straker-Squire in 1920 and the earlier part of 1921. He fell under the spell of the charm of Lionel Martin and his enthusiastic and perfectionist approach to motors, and, as Martin himself recalled.....''About this time there joined Aston-Martin Ltd., a long thin youth with a laugh no one could resist.....it was H. Kensington Moir — 'Albert' pronounced Frenchilly to us, we (my wife and I) 'Pa' and 'Ma' to him. He performed prodigies of tuning and resultant speed on the car(s), and while with us sowed the seeds of pit organisation which he later brought to full growth''.

Count Louis Vorow Zborowski was born in February 1895, the son of Count Eliot Zborowski and his wife Margaret, wealthy grand-daughter of William B. Astor. Born to an environment of wealth and sport (for Count Eliot Zborowski was a keen sportsman with a love of horses that was soon to be matched by an equally fervent passion for fast cars) it is not surprising that young 'Lou', as he was known to his friends, should have grown up with a natural flair for things mechanical. When young 'Lou' was eight years old his father was killed while driving his powerful Mercedes racing car in the La Turbie hill-climb in France, a sad blow which the boy felt deeply and which greatly altered the complexion of his life. Although outwardly ever the extrovert, those close to him knew that his 'wildness' and extravagant generosity masked an inner intellectualism and a deep sense of superstition that never left him.

He had spent two terms at Eton which had proved to be an unhappy episode in his life which was seldom if ever referred to, and by the beginning of the 1920s he had become keenly obsessed with motor cars and motor racing. Remembered by later generations chiefly for his rather wild 'tearabout' extrovertism and his succession of immense aero-engined racing cars, the legendary 'Chitty's', this too masked the fact that he was a truly dedicated racing driver of very real ability.

Working for and with Zborowski at his palatial country home at Higham, near Canterbury, was a friend of Zborowski's, one Clive Gallop, who had been an officer cadet at Sandhurst. Before the 1914-18 war he had been apprenticed as an engineer to the great French motor manufacturers, Peugeot, whose racing cars, designed by Ernest Henry, had really pioneered the modern conception of a high-efficiency twin-overhead camshaft engine of relatively small overall capacity, a design which had 'killed' the old monster racing cars of enormous litreage and which was to be developed into the fastest machinery of the next two decades. In being put through the mill with Peugeot Gallop came to have a detailed and thorough knowledge of the latest motor racing engineering practice and also to be on terms with the great racing drivers of the period — the brothers Boillot, Jules Goux, Zucarelli and others — who regularly drove for Peugeot.

After the war Gallop again concerned himself with motor racing and soon teamed up with Zborowski who was regularly racing his 'Chitty's', his ex-1914 Grand Prix Mercedes and his Ballot. To Gallop it seemed, as the regulations for the 1922 season were made known, that the only chance Zborowski might have of competing in some of the major events was by driving a small car, of which the rising new Aston-Martins seemed to hold forth the most prospects. So when Zborowski began taking a not disinterested look at the doings of the Aston-Martins at Brooklands he brought with him his friend Gallop. It was at this time that the two special track cars were being evolved at 53 Abingdon Road and the Robb 16-valve single overhead camshaft engine was taking shape.

More often than not Zborowski drove the ohc-engined track car and Kensington Moir the side-valver and this was in fact the case in the 1921 200-Miles Race, as we have seen. Zborowski's disappointment in the peformance of the car was echoed by Gallop and others and Zborowski's determination to drive an Aston-Martin in the forthcoming season (for he had been tremendously impressed by the handling and quality of the cars) with at least some hope of success urged him to put up some financial backing for the building of two new racing Astons which were to be fitted with new twin-overhead camshaft engines. He is alleged to have put up £10,000 but though we have it from Lionel Martin himself that Zborowski did indeed put some finance into the project at this time, there is no reliable record, it seems, of the precise amount involved.

One may wonder how it came about that Lionel Martin, seventeen years his senior, and, for all his sense of fun, a stickler for doing things 'according to the book', a man of impeccable manners but who could be icily polite to anyone to whom he wanted to give the brush-off, a man who was genuinely proud of his old school, Eton, at which he had been entirely happy, should have befriended the younger man, still only in his late twenties, who had always to cut a dash and whose behaviour was often as extravagant as his spending? Yet, allowing for the exuberance of Zborowski's youth and, perhaps, for the onset of middle age on Martin's side, there was much that they had in common apart from a mutual love of machinery and racing cars. Zborowski was an inveterate practical joker, just as Martin himself had been at the same age; beneath Zborowski's love of frenzied activity and pleasure there lay an astute, capable and intellectual mind. I doubt very much either would have for long tolerated the other had they not both recognised in the other very solid and sterling qualities. S.C.H. ('Sammy') Davis, who knew them both intimately, opines that the friendship — and the financial backing of the racing project — came about because Zborowski recognised in Martin "a bloke who would be a real friend".

And what of the plans for the production cars among all this racing activity? *The Autocar* Buyers' Guide for 1920, listing cars for 1921, had included the Aston-Martin but actual serious production was as far away as ever. 1921 was, for Aston-Martin, a year of constant competition activity which undoubtedly did much to cultivate the Aston-Martin name among knowledgeable enthusiasts and it was a year in which the seeds of future successes were sown, and as the year drew to a close to usher in 1922, 53 Abingdon Road, Kensington, was humming with even greater activity, but — the production cars existed on paper only. True, AM 270, the final prototype, had appeared in a number of relatively minor sprints, races and hill-climbs and other competitive events and had been driven some 12,000 miles including extensive testing on the Continent. Martin had taken the opportunity, since a trip to France was necessary to get 'Bunny' to Le Mans for the GP des Voiturettes, to take AM 270 with him and test the car in France and in the Alps, a fact referred to in *The Autocar's* Road Test that appeared in the issue of 8 October 1921. This report alluded to "the price of £850 for the car", which they then qualified by remarking ".....there is a double object in keeping the price high, since the output, naturally, is restricted both by the character of the car, which is at its best as a sporting model simply, and also because it is to be sold only, as it were, to the discerning few."

This last point had been recognised from the outset by Lionel Martin himself, who, in a letter to the motoring press two years earlier, had written ".....On the assumption that there is a market — if a limited one — for such a voiturette de luxe, I have laid my plans.....Whether I am right or wrong only time and my firm's pass-book can tell....."

Time was inexorably rolling on and the pass-book was taking a steady hammering and as yet no cars had been sold to the public. Such were the hard facts that must have dogged Lionel Martin's mind as the year 1922 dawned, but such was his belief, and that of his associates, in the rightness of his design and of the whole concept that their only thought was to press on with the project.

CHAPTER FOUR

One may be reasonably certain that if any one day was ringed in the Aston-Martin calendar for 1922 that day was Thursday 22 June.....the Tourist Trophy Race in the Isle of Man, target date for the first competitive outing for the two new twin-overhead camshaft 16-valve racing Aston-Martins on which Zborowski and Gallop were pinning their hopes, as indeed were all concerned in the Aston-Martin project. But in the rather perverse way that entries in one's diary tend to do, other dates were, in retrospect, to overshadow in importance those that one has underlined, circled or otherwise emphasised.

There had been no Tourist Trophy Race for cars since 1914 and the date selected for the 1922 event was a crucial one in the minds of others than Aston-Martin Ltd., for the experience and resources of Coatalen's STD combine were to be challenged by a portentous newcomer in the 3-litre class, the Bentley, and by a team of new Vauxhalls. Aston-Martin, of course, were concerned with the 1½-litre class, the 1500 Trophy, which was being run over 6 laps of the TT course as an adjunct to the main event. Here the Aston-Martins were certain to be challenged yet again by the 1½-litre Talbot-Darracqs, and if the latter's 1921 form was anything to go by, the challenger would indeed be a stiff one. So, what was being hatched at Abingdon Road was going to have to be a considerable advance on what had gone before if it was to be truly competitive.

And it was Gallop's Peugeot days that provided the inspiration. Peugeot had created a sensation way back in 1912 with their twin-overhead camshaft racing cars, a design that shortly was to set others feverishly making copies. Ernest Henry, of Peugeot, had removed himself to Ballot immediately after the war, but Marcel Gremillon was approached by Clive Gallop, with, of course, the backing of Zborowski and Martin, to design a new 1½-litre engine for the new Aston-Martin racers. What in effect he produced was virtually a half-size 3-litre Peugeot engine of Henry's design, or at least, the top half of it. Finance, it is said, dictated that the old Robb-designed bottom

60

half be married to the new top half and in fact the bore and stroke of the Robb and the Gremillon engines was the same. Alas, the new engines thus also inherited all the weaknesses of the Robb bottom half design met with already, but at least the new engines should put out a healthier bhp figure.

As for the rest of the car, the chassis was to be the shorter of the two lengths by then more or less established, and by dint of a powerful determination on Gallop's part to ensure that sets of Perrot four-wheel brakes were flown over from France as a strong hint that Aston-Martin should adopt them for the new racers, four-wheel brakes they did indeed have, and Rudge-Whitworth racing wire wheels to boot.

With the decision taken to enter for the 1500 Trophy and plans laid and work begun on the new cars it was prudent to take steps to survey the TT course, one of the most difficult in the world and famed already for the motorcycle events that went by the same title, the Tourist Trophy. Nobody in the Aston-Martin project had any first-hand experience of the course or conditions, and since previous motor-car TTs had not catered for cars of less than 1500cc (which in any case had improved out of all recognition since the last TT in 1914), the course offered no yardstick in this class.

So in the very early months of 1922 the 'Aston-Martin Boys' took a road-equipped Aston-Martin racer, wearing the registration mark AM 273 (familiar the previous season as a track car and in sprints) over to the Isle of Man. The 'AM Boys' in question were Lionel Martin himself, Clive Gallop, Bertie Kensington Moir and Lou Zborowski. The weather they experienced might almost have put them off, for snow lay so thick on the mountain road from Ramsey round the notorious hairpin and The Gooseneck that when the car returned to Ramsey snow lay tightly packed in the artillery wheels and along the running-boards. Nevertheless the expedition was a profitable one and they learned a great deal. Snow on the Island.....and June must have seemed far away!

Much closer at hand, however, was Kensington Moir's next episode with the irrepressible 'Bunny', for on 15 February he succeeded in lowering the record for the Brooklands Test Hill to 9·29 seconds, a speed of 25·85mph, thus temporarily relieving Capt. Archie Frazer-Nash's G.N. of the record — temporarily because Frazer-Nash managed to better this figure substantially before the year was out. Moir topped the hill at 40mph at 4,200rpm in bottom gear, and his success with 'Bunny' was excellent publicity material and prompted Lionel Martin to take whole-page illustrated advertisements in the motoring press. As was customary in any Aston-Martin enterprise, the whole episode took on a family party atmosphere with Lionel and Katherine much in evidence. So too was a dapper little man in overcoat and bowler hat who was alleged to have been subsequently charged with murder, but that does not really concern the Aston-Martin story — he just happened to be in camera range in the odd photograph!

Work on the two TT cars was going ahead, the entries for the race had been made and April ticked on into May, the great day in the diary looming more urgently now. But May brought some outstanding kudos to the firm for, as Martin himself recorded in later years — ".....it occurred to me that no 'light' car, e.g. one under 1500cc, had ever broken a world's record". Accordingly detailed arrangements were made to gather together a team of drivers and to book the track at Brooklands for 24/25 May. The car to be used for this historic attempt was none other than 'Bunny' and the team of drivers were S.C.H. Davis, Clive Gallop and 'Bertie' Kensington Moir. Quite apart from any contingency that might arise during the actual running of the car, Martin realised that efficient pit routine for the replenishment stops that would be needed would play a vital part in the success or otherwise of the attempt and the most meticulous practice was planned and carried out, Martin himself taking on the responsibility of refuelling the car. 'Sammy' Davis recalls of this occasion; "When we drove for him he gave us a personal friendship rare in 'the trade' though, again, he would stand no excuses from his drivers however ingenious they might be. You had to do a job of work and do it well. He took a profound interest in the strategy of a record attempt, planning every move of everyone during a refill, and, as 'Bunny's' famous world records proved, calmly misleading his opponents who were running for records at the same time".

The opponents in this instance were A.C., a rival light car that at this period was a frequent contender for the 1½-litre honours in races, sprints and hill-climbs. The fact that both cars were out on the track together added considerable spice to the occasion. 'Bunny' led off at the early hour of 4.30am on this fine but misty May morning, a morning that promised a day of hot sunshine as indeed turned out to be the case. During the whole of that day through the scorching heat the two cars, Aston-Martin and A.C., flew round the track, lapping at over 80mph as records fell. The scheduled stops were moments of intense activity and soon attracted spectators, Katherine Martin being present at nearly all of them, and in addition to Martin's own mechanics and Jack Addis, the Works foreman, representatives of the oil company and of Shell, together with Raynham, manager of the nearby and well-known hostelry 'The Hand and Spear', were present at some of the stops.

By 7·00pm the A.C. had come in for the last time, a number of Light Car records to its credit, and was officially sealed and locked away for the night before resuming on the morrow. 'Bunny' and the Aston-Martin personnel, hot, tired, dusty but delighted, continued with their record attempt, much to the astonishment of the A.C. camp. Finally at 9·20pm 'Bunny' too came in for the last time, the entire assembly cheering wildly. That long, hot and weary day had brought ten World's Records and 22 Light-Car class records as well as reward. 'Bunny' had certainly earned a reputation that was to become legendary in the annals of motor sport.

Tremendous fillip though this was, the TT was now less than a month away and problems were beginning to threaten the readiness of the two TT cars being specially prepared. Incidentally, though these cars have subsequently become known as the 'G.P.' or 'Strasbourg' cars, a great deal of confusion has arisen in later years over the precise identity of each, a confusion worse confounded through Martin's habit of freely exchanging registration numbers, already referred to. A surer identification is the fact that many of the major components of the two cars built for the 1922 TT (and which became entries for the French G.P. at Strasbourg also) were stamped 'TT1' or 'TT2', though over the years some of these components have found their way on to other chassis.

The first of the twin-cam TT cars was registered as XL 2445 on 9 June, (for they were to be driven to Liverpool and thence to the Isle of Man), but the second car not until 19 June, a bare three days before the race, when it was registered XL 3125. After all this feverish work and preparation, Martin recalled many years later that it was with delight that he and Katherine watched the cars set off for Liverpool, but he was doomed to disappointment. Gallop and Zborowski were to have driven the cars in the 1500 Trophy, but alas, the preparation had been too rushed and the cars had to be withdrawn. Unwilling to bow out entirely and allow the make to be unrepresented in the race, Kensington Moir and 'Bunny' were hastily brought to the rescue. 'Bunny' had had no special attention since her World's Records bid almost a month previously and, sadly, did not complete the race, going out with a broken valve spring, complicated by the fact that the valve cap could not be shifted to replace it, the side-valve engines having a fixed head. The whole event turned out to be an STD benefit, Sunbeam winning the Tourist Trophy itself while the 1500 Trophy was won by a Talbot-Darracq, with another in second place and a Bugatti in third position.

The trip back from the Island must have been a disappointing one for the supporters of Aston-Martin, for the make's first appearance on Manx soil had been a sorry contrast to that of the Bentley equipe, whose three cars had acquitted themselves most creditably on their first major race outing on British soil. And it was on the return journey aboard the Isle of Man Steam Packet Co's "Castle Mona" that an introduction was made that was to have considerable significance not only in the affairs of Aston-Martin but also in those of that other rising British sporting car, the Bentley. As W.O. Bentley himself recalls, it was then that he was introduced to 'Bertie' Kensington Moir and just as Lionel Martin had been earlier, found himself greatly impressed by this young man full of fun, energy and charm. W.O. Bentley recalls that they talked for the rest of the trip and far into the night, and the upshot of this meeting was that Moir was invited to join the Bentley concern, an offer which he accepted. However, Moir drove for Aston-Martin on many other occasions during 1922 before taking up his new post with Bentley Motors.

Still the new Aston-Martin racers remained unblooded. Zborowski's other 'target' for the cars was, of course, the French Grand Prix to be held at Strasbourg on 15 July. Prior to that, however, the cars were entered for the South Hants AC's Spread Eagle hill-climb to be held on 1 July; Moir and Zborowski with the overhead camshaft cars and Martin himself with a side-valver. Only a fortnight ahead was the great day of the French GP. One must remember that to take a team of cars to Continental events in those days was a very different undertaking from doing the same thing to-day; no air ferries or chartered aircraft, no giant transporters to render the task speedy and virtually self-contained. If one was not prepared to risk the complications and hazards of train and ship with all the attendant loading and unloading, the possibility — indeed probability in some countries — of loss or damage and all the worries of minor officialdom, then the only choice was to drive the cars on the road for the whole journey apart from the sea trip. However lightheartedly such a road trip may have been undertaken (and to the present generation the very notion of being allowed to take a Grand Prix car on the road legally must seem light-hearted in the extreme), much careful organisation would be required.

A trip of this nature was just what Lionel Martin revelled in. He was an experienced Continental motorist as we have seen, and his flair for and love of the most meticulous planning of routes, mileages and all the likely contingencies could really come to the fore. With Zborowski and Gallop to drive the race cars and Martin and the mechanics accompanying them, the cars were driven to the Channel ports and thence across Northern France to

34. Kensington Moir at the wheel of one of the track cars. Among the spectators are Capt. 'Archie' Frazer-Nash (2nd from left) and Humphrey Cook (4th from left), while Jack Addis leans on the tail

35. A shot which well reveals the beautiful shape of the long-tailed track car in its polished aluminium finish

36. 'Coal Scuttle' with Victor
Bruce at Brooklands, 1921
200-Miles Race

37. A close-up of a smiling
Kensington Moir at the wheel of the
long-tailed track car, flanked by
Lionel Martin and Jack Addis

38. Zborowski at the wheel of the
long-tailed track car at Brooklands.
Note the 'separate' radiator and the
ram-pipe for the carburettor intake.
Why was the wheelbrace left sculling?

39. Divided loyalties? Zborowski in
the 2-ohc Strasbourg car at Shelseley
in 1922 and . . .

40. . . . his ex-Indianapolis Ballot (no. 19) in the top paddock at the same event nestles alongside 'Bunny' (no. 22) which Kensington Moir had driven up the hill in 57.2 sec

41. Lionel Martin takes the final prototype AM270 up Kop Hill in one of the many events held there prior to the RAC's ban in 1925

42. W.G. Barlow in his side-valve short-chassis GP replica with road equipment. This car was delivered to Barlow in February 1923 and was raced by him with some success before eventually becoming the basis of the Halford Special. Photographed in the summer of 1923

43. Private owner's success; R.C. Morgan in 'Green Pea' cornering during the GP de Boulogne in September 1923. Mrs Marion Agnew was his riding mechanic and they finished second to Segrave's Talbot-Darracq

44. Photographed after the finish . . .

45. . . . and with the legend 'Petit Pois' clearly visible and the dirt of the race still proudly borne, the object of interested scrutiny in the street

46. Fun on the sands at Porthcawl; 'Bunny' (left, No. 19) and AM270 (No. 16) with Lionel Martin at the wheel

47. 'Bunny' matched against N.T. Beardsell's Hodgson at a Blackpool speed event

48. Capt. George Eyston drifts the 'wrongly-numbered' ex-Gallop 2-ohc Strasbourg car during a hill-climb

BAMFORD & MARTIN, LIMITED.

—

ENGINEERS.

—

TELEPHONE: WESTERN 4003.
TELEGRAMS: ASTOMARTIA, KENS, LONDON.

—

MANUFACTURERS OF
THE ASTON-MARTIN CAR.

53, ABINGDON ROAD,

KENSINGTON,

LONDON, W. 8.

R. C. Morgan, Esq.,
Old Hatch Farm,
Abinger Hammer,
Near Dorking.

2nd July, 1924.

Dear Mr. Morgan,

  Your long racer will be ready to-morrow morning first thing.

  You already have the invoice for the work, and as the amount is such a large one, and we, as you know are running on our private means, I should be very much obliged if you would let us have your cheque when you collect your car.

    Yours faithfully,

    Lionel Martin.

CARS DRIVEN ONLY AT CLIENTS' OWN RISK AND RESPONSIBILITY.

49 and 50 (overleaf). Facsimile of letters written from Lionel Martin to R.C. Morgan. The invoice refers to work done on Morgan's long-tailed track car that he crashed at South Harting at the beginning of June, 1924

BAMFORD & MARTIN, LIMITED.

ENGINEERS.

—

TELEPHONE: WESTERN 4003.
TELEGRAMS: ASTOMARTIA, KENS, LONDON.

—

MANUFACTURERS OF
THE ASTON-MARTIN CAR.

53, ABINGDON ROAD,

KENSINGTON,

LONDON, W. 8.

INVOICE.

R. C. Morgan, Esq.,
Old Hatch Farm,
Abinger Hammer,
Surrey.

26th June, 1924.

Dr to BAMFORD & MARTIN, LIMITED.

To Dismantling chassis of all parts.
" Straightening chassis, cleaning, painting and re-assembling all parts.
" Dismantling front axle, straightening axle beam, cleaning and re-assembling all parts.
" Straightening tie rod cam, steering drop arm, tie and push rods.
" Dismantling front road springs, cleaning, examining and re-setting.
" Cleaning and examining rear road springs.
" Dismantling rear axle, cleaning, examining, straightening differ-ential cases, supplying and fitting 2 axle sleeves, making and fitting one special axle shaft and re-assembling.
" Dismantling gear box, cleaning, examining fitting new bushes to universal joint and re-assembling.
" Repairing starting dog housing on engine.
" Supplying and fitting one starting handle complete less grip
"   "   "   "   one front cross member complete with all fittings.

	£.	s.	d.
	65.	19.	9.

Material supplied for above repair.

		£.	s.	d.
1	Starting handle complete less grip.	1.	3.	9.
1	Front cross member	4.	9.	2.
2	Rear axle sleeves	15.	2.	0.
1	" " shaft.	5.	0.	0.
3	Steering arms	2.	14.	0.

51. Spanish interlude: Zborowski with the 2-ohc car (No. 6) prior to the start of the Penya Rhin GP, 1923. An Elizalde and a Chiribiri left and right in the foreground

52. Zborowski in the Aston-Martin passes the grandstand and pits in the same event

53. A close-up of an earnest discussion with Zborowski, who finished in second place, immediately after the race. This is the car that had been registered as **XP 3037** in September 1923

54. November sun in Spain at the newly opened Sitges track. The 2-ohc Aston-Martin (No. 5), still showing signs of its Penya Rhin number 6, alongside Zborowski's Miller (No. 9)

55.   Gallop in the Aston (No.
5) heads Zborowski in the
Miller as they pass the stands at
Sitges, 1923

56. Sitges, 1923. Gallop,
Zborowski and Lionel Martin
snapped inside the Aston-
Martin pit

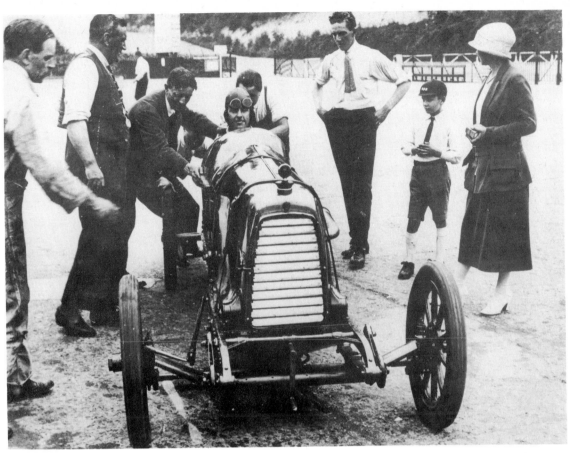

57. Debut for 'Razorblade', 1923. Capt. Frank Halford at the wheel is watched by Lionel Martin (2nd left) and Katherine Martin (right). John Martin, as a schoolboy, is an enthralled spectator

58. A modern shot of the superb restoration of 'Razorblade' by the late F.E. Ellis emphasises how cleverly the design was slimmed down. Although originally fitted with Sankey artillery wheels, wire knock-offs were used from late 1924

59. (opposite top). Lionel and Katherine Martin take AM 270 in her final form (fwb and wire wheels) up Simms Hill, Devonshire

60. (opposite bottom). Lionel and Katherine Martin (extreme left) in the paddock at Shelsley Walsh in September 1923. In the centre Leslie Wilson is in discussion with Capt. 'Archie' Frazer-Nash

61. A sea change! XP 3037 after the crash and rebuild, portrayed at Higham, Zborowki's Kentish home. The car shows by the odd angle of the rear spring shackles, the difficulty experienced in aligning the propshaft and axle in the new chassis, and is painted in Zborowski's characteristic white

62. XP 3037 in later years, after the 'Sajito' rebuild. It is shown here in 'Mort' Morris-Goodall's hands in an MCC Exeter Trial

63. No. 1928, registered DM 2986, a side-valve car purchased brand-new by R.F. Summers, is portrayed here outside the Birmingham works of the coachbuilders W.C. & R.C. Atcherley . . . and a very pretty body it is

64. The same car again, portrayed ascending Shelsley Walsh in 1924

65. No. 1937, a side-valve long chassis tourer supplied brand-new in 1924 to Capt. The Revd Herbert Ward. It was fitted with a Jarvis-built two-seater sports body in the following year while still in Capt. Ward's ownership

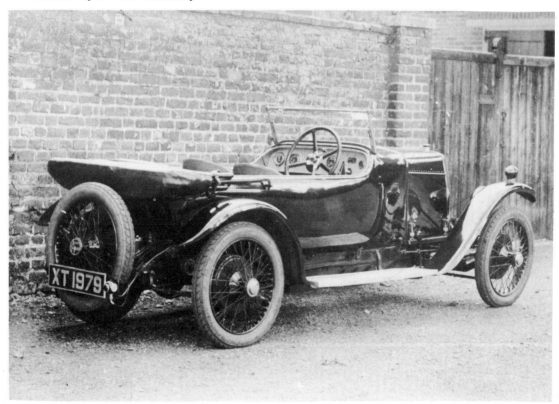

66.   DM 2986, R.F. Summer's car, also underwent a change of body when only a few months old, the builder of this one being Compton & Hermon, of Hersham. It was finished in mottled aluminium and is seen here with the owner at the wheel . . .

67.   . . . and here at the Essex MC Open event at Kop on 29 March 1924 . . .

68. . . . and here with some worthy opposition at the Whitsun Meeting, Brooklands, 1924 in the Private Competitors Handicap. It is second from the right in the rear

Strasbourg. Other British entries, the Sunbeams, were doing the same thing, as Segrave recalled of the Wolverhampton entry.

Of the race itself, run with all the pomp, ceremony and excitement that characterise such events on the Continent, the outcome was somewhat chastening for the British entries, both Sunbeams and Aston-Martins. The latter gave away some half-litre in capacity, the limit being 2-litres, and had to carry extra weight to comply with the regulations. Many years later Lionel Martin recalled of this; ".....for the *pesage* nothing could be added to the cars and we weighed too light. A kind-hearted official told us to come back again after lunch, and in the meantime, to make sure that nothing important had been omitted from the cars. After lunch we were heavy enough!" However, the cars were achieving some 94mph on the course and by half-distance Gallop was holding 5th place in No. 8 and Zborowski was 6th in No. 15. At this juncture Zborowski was forced to retire with magneto maladies and after continuing to run well in 5th position for some time Gallop too had to retire due to broken valve springs. It was a blow to Aston-Martin hopes that both cars had had to retire, but they had shown their potential and had put up a very creditable performance in the earlier stages of the race.

Back in Britain, Zborowski had entered both his 4·9-litre 1919 ex-Indianapolis Ballot and the twin-cam Aston that he had driven at Strasbourg for the Midland AC's famous Shelsley Walsh hill-climb to be held at that picturesque Worcestershire venue on 29 July, little enough time to make the return journey from Strasbourg and to check and prepare the Aston. Lionel Martin had entered three other Aston-Martins for the Shelsley climb, Moir with the ever-versatile 'Bunny' and his wife and himself with side-valvers. The Shelsley crowd, many of them aware of Zborowski's vivid reputation, expected great things of him, both with the Ballot and the Aston, but with the latter, alas, his time was less impressive than the splendid dustcloud that he raised on the corners, for he could not better a time of 61·8 seconds, whereas Moir managed an impressive 57·2 with 'Bunny' to win the Light Car class. Zborowski's car carrying the number 30 still bore its Strasbourg number 15 painted on the scuttle and the radiator stoneguard and carried the index number XL2445 as it had done in France prior to the race.

Mrs Kensington Moir recalled to the author many years later that she accompanied Zborowski in the GP car to Shelsley on this occasion. She remarked that the shock absorbers were tight and the journey was "absolute hell" and not only because Zborowski always took the most appalling risks! This very eventful season found the Astons being prepared next for the

JCC's second 200-Miles Race at Brooklands, an event again very well supported after its initial success the previous year and at which the Talbot-Darracq team were again to be present. Zborowski and Moir were each to drive one of the twin-cam cars and C.G. Stead was to drive that incredible car 'Bunny' with a tuned side-valve engine. This event was to take place on 19 August and was already the cause of much comment and speculation in the motoring press.

Stead in 'Bunny' actually led the field away in the 1½-litre race, which started at 2·00pm, and Moir in the ex-Gallop Strasbourg car then pushed to the front, gaining nearly half a lap lead. By the second lap, however, two of the Talbot-Darracqs and Zborowski in the other twin-cam Aston were close on his heels. The twin-cam Astons had been lapping consistently with the Talbot-Darracqs at around 94mph in practice and the Aston-Martin chances seemed set fair. But alas, the dreaded magneto ailment again caused Moir's retirement, soon to be followed by that of Zborowski from the same cause. It was now left to Stead and 'Bunny' only to uphold the Aston-Martin flag and that they both did most nobly, Stead eventually bringing 'Bunny' home to second place behind the Talbot-Darracq of Guinness and ahead of Segrave's similar car. The remaining car of the Talbot-Darracq team, that of Chassagne, had unfortunately crashed, luckily without injury to Chassagne or his mechanic. Of Chassagne's crash, in which the Talbot-Darracq plunged over the Byfleet banking and Chassagne and his mechanic Dutoit were thrown clear, Mrs Moir recalls that she was waiting with her husband beside his Aston-Martin (which had retired earlier with magneto trouble) and helped to pick thorns from Chassagne's feet and legs, for he had had his shoes pulled off when flung out of the car. The shoes were found neatly 'parked' beside the track. Stead's average speed for the race was 86·35mph, while that of Guinness was 88·06mph, an amazing feat for 'Bunny' to have achieved.

I am indebted to R. Dallas Brett, OBE, for the following account of the excitement and tension that engulfed the Aston-Martin pit as the race drew towards its end. Dallas Brett was a spectator at this event and was placed immediately behind the Aston-Martin pit, where a heated argument was going on between Lionel and Katherine Martin as to whether 'Bunny' should be recalled for fuel, for it was touch and go that 'Bunny', going flat out in the hope of fending off Segrave in one of the Talbot-Darracqs and who had now speeded up considerably, might not last out. Lionel wanted to play safe and refuel 'Bunny', with the likelihood that if he did so Segrave would take second place, while Katherine was all for taking an all-or-nothing risk that 'Bunny's' fuel would last out and that Stead would just manage to hold off Segrave. Katherine won the day and 'Bunny' was not brought in, but Segrave was visibly gaining, lapping at 100mph to Stead's 87mph. The entire personnel of the Aston-Martin pit was aloft on the tin roof of the pit watching 'Bunny's' progress through field glasses and straining every ear for the dread sound of 'Bunny's' engine cutting out for lack of fuel. Just as Stead pulled the car off the banking before the Fork 'Bunny's' engine coughed and died, and the car coasted, engine dead and silent, over the line, with Segrave in the Talbot-Darracq fifty yards astern to cross the line at 100mph. But ... second place *was* 'Bunny's' and a tremendous ovation greeted Stead.

Despite such a busy season Lionel Martin and the 'AM Boys' contrived to put in some hectic and enjoyable week-end motoring in which competition in the motoring sense was a fierce as ever, even if unofficial. Lionel and Katherine Martin, having enjoyed much hospitality at Zborowski's country house at Higham.....hospitality not unmixed with uproarious practical joking.....decided to invite Lou and the Countess (Countess Zborowska, formerly Violet Leicester, whom he had married in 1919), together with Clive Gallop and another of Zborowski's extrovert motoring friends Major 'Shuggar' Cooper, to spend a week-end at a Sidmouth hotel. Martin's account of the adventures and misadventures, and the various junketings on the road and off it, make entertaining reading and appeared in a long article from his pen which appeared in *Motor Sport* in 1944. At the time Zborowski had on trial the ex-Indianapolis Ballot that he subsequently bought and which he first entered at a Brooklands event in the Private Competitors Handicap of Easter 1922.

Sidmouth was a resort much favoured by Lionel and Katherine Martin and they frequently motored there, often accompanied by friends who could well be described as high-spirited, and who would 'play hell' in the 'posh' hotels. No doubt there were many raised eyebrows, perhaps not a few injured dignities, but Zborowski, whom Martin referred to as 'a prince of sportsmen', could be as charming in manner as could Martin himself and it is unlikely that many took permanent offence.

Zborowski had entered his twin-cam car for the Grand Prix de Penya Rhin at Barcelona which was to be held on 5 November 1922. Despite the date the weather was fine, warm and sunny for the race which attracted an enormous crowd of spectators. Among them was no less a personage than the King of Spain, Alfonso XIII, a perfervid motoring enthusiast, who watched the whole event from the Royal box. The fifteen starters were comprised of seven makes, and among them the highly successful Talbot-Darracqs. Zborowski's Aston-Martin was out among the leaders very early in the race, fighting it out with one of the Talbot-Darracqs and a Chiribiri. Guinness in a Talbot-Darracq managed to establish a lead and Segrave came up into a challenging position, duelling hard with Zborowski in the Aston until trouble overtook him with the final result that Guinness came home the victor and Zborowski brought the Aston-Martin in to second place, a most creditable performance and one in which, luckily, the magneto maladies for once had been absent.

Apart from the Spread Eagle event which saw the twin-cam Astons in competition for the first time, no mention has been made of the many similar sprints and hill-climbs at which the other Works cars were frequent competitors in this busy season. The staff at 53 Abingdon Road must have been very fully occupied indeed to keep the cars serviced and prepared for all this activity and one may well ask again what progress, if any, was being made towards production.

Lionel Martin's fascinating account in *Motor Sport* of November 1944 reveals the fact that even in the early part of 1922 at the time when Zborowski and friends joined him in the Sidmouth trip, a journey was made to Bristol to try to persuade the principals of 'an aeroplane firm' to undertake the task of putting the Aston-Martin into production. The trip from Sidmouth to Bristol was made in the Ballot and 'Bunny'. The Ballot stalled repeatedly and a convenient bystander was not always to hand to give the car a push start so the party arrived late for lunch. Various other minor misadventures rather spoiled the harmony of the occasion, which Martin summed up by saying, "altogether the visit to Bristol was not a success" and nothing came of the attempt to get the Astons into production in this way. But the episode is revealing in that it shows that Martin, even as early as that, was keenly aware of the difficulties that getting any production cars built would inevitably bring. A whole year had again almost gone by since the problem had loomed acutely even before the work on the new twin-camshaft racers had begun. 1922 had certainly brought renown for the make but honest reflection must have admitted that this was largely due to 'Bunny's' exploits rather than to the introduction of the twin-cam racers. True, these had shown great potential but as yet lacked the reliability of the side-valve units. Again, by far the lion's share of the successful racing and sprint performances had been put up by Kensington Moir and he was about to leave the firm and move on to Bentley Motors as second-in-command of their service department. So the closing weeks of 1922 must again have been a time for a hard and honest re-appraisal of the course that the Company was to take.

One name noticeably absent from the account of the firm's activities is that of Robert Bamford who had, it will be remembered, been joint founder with Lionel Martin in 1912. He seems to have lost interest in the project and one of the last photographs of him as part of the Company shows him with Martin and Kensington Moir grouped around AM 270, the final prototype, and he left the firm around this time. Lionel Martin bought out his share and Katherine Martin was officially appointed a director in Bamford's place.

CHAPTER FIVE

The very closing days of 1922 reveal the fact that after only some six months of use the disposal of the twin-cam Zborowski/Gallop-inspired racers into private ownership was in the wind. In December 1922 Martin was approached by R.C. Morgan who wanted one of these cars. Martin telephoned to Morgan on 29 December, and confirmed this telephone call by letter dated 1 January 1923, to say that he would sell 'No. 9' (the car that Zborowski had raced at Penya Rhin in November), but fitted with side-valve engine and road-equipped with light wings and a three-lamp lighting set. Morgan had already inspected the car and was evidently satisfied with Martin's suggestions, for on 29 January 1923 a deposit for the car was paid and acknowledged. This car, which had been registered XL 2445 on 9 June 1922, was, however, delivered to Morgan wearing the registration plates of the other (Gallop) car, XL 3125, a fact of which Morgan and his wife remained in ignorance for over fifty years!

In February 1923 a similar car with side-valve engine was delivered to W.G. Barlow who had earlier raced one of the ex-1914 TT Humbers at Brooklands and who then had and raced an early 3-litre Bentley. So, at last, some Aston-Martins were getting into private hands. Indeed, J.S. Robertson, Bamford & Martin Ltd's Secretary, had a rear-wheel braked artillery-wheeled all-weather (apparently more out of a sense of duty to the firm rather than from any inclinations as a sporting driver) which featured in the Aston-Martin catalogue long after fwb and Rudge wire wheels were the normal wear. A close friend of Martin's, a Mr Greenall, who was a Lloyds Insurance Broker, had the first production fwb car, No. 1919, which was also an all-weather model. On 27 March 1923 Car No. 1918 which had been used by the Works for racing and sprint events, with a side-valve engine and also two-wheel braked with artillery wheels, was sold to Capt. J.C. Douglas of 71B Sinclair Road, Kensington, W14. Douglas was a motoring correspondent and racing motorist and was much associated with Aston-Martins over the following two to three years. This Aston, registered XN 2902 and nicknamed 'Nigger' is fortunately still extant though much modified.

92

On 20 July 1923 'Nigger' was sold, or perhaps transferred, to Katherine Martin's ownership, for by this time Douglas had taken delivery of a long-chassis tourer with wire wheels and fwb, Car No. 1920, which many many years later was owned by the author. Three further cars, all side-valvers, were sold to private owners during the year and "production", albeit on a minute scale, could be said to have begun. Mrs Martin, incidentally, retained ownership of 'Nigger' until 20 May 1924 by which time Capt. Douglas was increasingly concerned with racing other Aston-Martins.

The second of the twin-ohc cars (that raced by Gallop at Strasbourg) had been disposed of to Capt. G.E.T. Eyston, strangely enough also, on account of the change of registration numbers that took place when Morgan took delivery of the ex-Zborowski car, wearing a "wrong" number.....XL 2445.....a confusion that has made the task of later historians somewhat more difficult! When Eyston bought the GP car 'wrongly' registered XL 2445 he also bought the 1922 200-Miles track car. The 2-ohc engine from the GP car was removed and used in 'Razorblade' and the 2-ohc engine from the track car was used in it or the GP car as occasion demanded.

If "production" was minimal during 1923 competition appearances were by contrast as frequent as before. As far as Brooklands events were concerned it was notable that an entirely new string of names replaced the Aston drivers of the previous season. Prominent among these were Eyston and Morgan with the two ex-Strasbourg cars, Morgan's now sporting the name 'Green Pea' on the bonnet. Both Capt. Douglas and W.G. Barlow competed in a number of events, the former with the side-valver 'Nigger', the latter with his short-chassis side-valver with GP body, registered OR 1. Morgan's first competition appearance with 'Green Pea' had been, surprisingly perhaps, in the MCC's London-Land's-End Trial in which he gained a gold medal and drove in company with Lionel and Mrs Martin with the up-dated AM 270.....up-dated in that this car now wore wire wheels and fwb. 'Green Pea's' first Brooklands outing in Morgan's hands was at the Midsummer Meeting of 1923, but his entry, as far as Aston-Martins were concerned, was overshadowed by the appearance of a very specialised and novel Aston built for a specific purpose which, alas, it did not achieve. This car was a twin-overhead camshaft-engined single-seater of exceptionally narrow track and body width of only 18½" overall. Markedly crab-tracked, the rear track being only 3ft., front track of 4ft., the differential-less back axle was carried on very short, stiff quarter-elliptic springs and the very small metal-to-metal rear brakes were ex-Singer Ten and virtually useless. Fitted with a beautifully streamlined body intended originally to have an all-enveloping cockpit (which was later abandoned), this car was designed with the express intent of

93

becoming the first Light Car to exceed 100 miles in the hour. It was brought to the line at the Midsummer Meeting for the 90mph Short Handicap in the hands of Major F.B. Halford and according to *The Autocar* was nicknamed 'The Oyster' but this nickname seems to have very soon given place to that by which the car has always subsequently been known.....'Razorblade'. It proved a difficult car to handle and also prone to throwing its off-side front tyre when at Brooklands. In early days this car wore steel artillery wheels, the front axle being brakeless but smoothly streamlined with shaped wooden fairings and a full-length undershield was fitted. During 1924 it acquired wire wheels of racing pattern but still lacked fwb. Naturally its debut at the track was of the utmost concern to Lionel Martin, and he and his wife Katherine and his son John, then aged ten, are portrayed in one of the illustrations, with Halford at the wheel and the Works Foreman, Jack Addis, beside the car. It went well, lapping at 98.04mph but it was obvious that a number of problems still needed to be ironed out. However, it did pull off a win in the 100mph Short Handicap at 99.81mph from Ropner's 30/98 Vauxhall.

While Eyston and Halford continued to appear regularly with the Astons at Brooklands events R.C. Morgan with 'Green Pea' managed to gain one first, two second and four third places in 1923 at Brooklands races, thus perhaps emphasising side-valve reliability. All these drivers appeared also at various sprint events up and down the country and were attended with a certain degree of success. E.R. Hall was also still campaigning the veteran 'Bunny' to good effect. This car appeared at Shelsley Walsh on 8 September in Hall's hands, at which event there appeared also Miss Winifred Pink from Taunton driving AM 270 with Lionel Martin himself as an energetic passenger. Miss Pink was a regular competitor at sprint events such as Shelsley, Caerphilly, Angel Bank, Kop and Porthcawl, usually competing in the Ladies' and Formula classes where these were available and frequently gaining awards.....all good for the Aston name.

R.C. Morgan with 'Green Pea' achieved a notable success in the Boulogne GP des Voiturettes in September 1923 by bringing this private entry into 2nd place behind the maestro Segrave with one of the Talbot-Darracqs. Acting as riding mechanic to Morgan on this occasion, as on so many others, was Mrs Marion Agnew (later Mrs Morgan). For them the closing laps of the race were fraught with excitement and maddening misadventure. Their Aston was using Englebert tyres and in this event they were trying out a new Englebert jack supplied by the firm. A wheel change was called for in the closing stages of the race and Morgan brought the car into the pits. Segrave was well ahead but Benoist in a Salmson running in the 1100cc class was lapping well and leading his class. The wheel change completed on Morgan's Aston, to Mrs Agnew's horror the new Englebert jack jammed in the raised position and all her efforts failed to release it. Eagerly the crowd surged round, all eager to help push the car off the jack and Mrs Agnew had a very difficult task to persuade the gallant Frenchmen not to touch the car as this would have resulted in its disqualification. Eventually it was possible to roll and bump the Aston off the jack, Morgan attempted a roll start on the slight downgrade but 'Green Pea' (also bearing the legend 'Petit Pois' for French edification and delight) refused to start. Mrs Agnew knew that the downgrade soon gave way to a slight upgrade and that she would never be able to continue pushing up that. In the nick of time she noticed that Morgan had not switched the ignition on and this was remedied and the Aston started and was away! But in all this delay Benoist in the Salmson had slipped by so that although the Aston-Martin was correctly credited with 2nd place to Segrave, Morgan had been third to cross the finishing line, the Salmson winning the smaller capacity event. In the confusion and haste of that last getaway the faulty jack and the discarded spare wheel had been flung to the side of the track from which spot an annoyed and disgruntled Englebert representative, a Dutchman, Meuhlen-kamp, always smartly dressed and be-ringed, was told he might fetch them. To add further honours for the make, George Eyston brought his Aston-Martin in to 3rd place behind Morgan.

As the autumn drew in to October attention was all focussed once again on the now well-established JCC 200-Miles Race at Brooklands, to be held on Saturday 13 October. By the close of entries at ordinary fees four Astons were listed but as the practice days neared, Lionel Martin realised that he could not use two of his entries and sportingly gave them to Henly's, the Alvis entrants, who had unwittingly overlooked the closing date. Eyston's mechanic, Gillow, got the Eyston 2-ohc car round at some 98mph in practice, but two of the other entries were not even ready, and the Astons that had turned out to practise proved to be too noisy for the authorities and were sent away to improve their silencing arrangements.

At last the great day came and it was Hall in 'Bunny', now endowed with 16-valve 2-ohc engine, that followed Cushman's Bugatti away from the start in the 1½-litre class, Hall in turn followed by Harvey's Alvis, the ultimate winner. The Talbot-Darracqs that had proved invincible in the previous 200-Miles Races were not entered, for fear, so it was said, of being trounced by the much-favoured Fiats entered from Italy and driven by Salamano and Malcolm Campbell. Although very fast these two proved to be somewhat damp squibs for they retired in the 11th and 12th laps respectively. Eyston's

Aston-Martin led at one stage but dropped back and slowed when assailed by a malady that was eventually cured when Eyston decided at last to change the plugs! Harvey's Alvis now had an almost unassailable lead, while behind him Eyston tried with all his skill to make up for his earlier slow laps. Fastest lap was a tie between Joyce's AC and Eyston in the Aston-Martin at 99·51mph, but Eyston, despite this, could not better 4th position, with R.C. Morgan's ex-Zborowski car in the 6th place and E.R. Hall, who had suffered tyre trouble with 'Bunny', coming in 9th.

There remained the Spanish events at Penya Rhin, Barcelona and the new 'concrete saucer' at Sitges in November. Zborowski had taken over his recently acquired Miller and an Aston-Martin (XP 3037). At Penya Rhin the Aston-Martin, wearing the racing No. 6 and driven by Zborowski had managed 2nd place, 3m.27s. behind Divo (Talbot-Darracq) and more than half-an-hour ahead of Resta, the opposition being of much the same calibre as it had been in 1922 when he had also achieved 2nd place (to Kenelm Lee Guinness in one of the Talbot-Darracqs). Sitges was a new venue, the track but newly opened and still in a barely finished state. Here Gallop drove the Aston-Martin, now with the racing number 5 and Zborowski piloted the Miller, painted in Zborowski's customary white and carrying the racing number 9. In this event the Aston-Martin managed a 3rd place behind the Talbot-Darracqs of Resta and Divo.

The year was drawing to an end — 1924 was on the horizon. And what a baffling and paradoxical year it was destined to be! In terms of production it was to be the firm's best year, with 26 cars, Nos. 1924 — 1949 inclusive, leaving the little Kensington works. Although *The Autocar* had stated when it illustrated the short-chassis side-valve car supplied to W.G. Barlow in February 1923 that Capt. Malcolm Campbell had been appointed London agent, he seems to have sold few if any Aston-Martins, for by 1924 and subsequently it was G.L. Francis & Co., of 169 Shaftesbury Avenue, and later of 110 Great Portland Street who advertised themselves as London agents for the Aston-Martin, and indeed, a study of the "smalls" in the motoring press of the time reveals that the majority appear to have been sold through this firm.

In April 1924 Aston-Martin prices were advertised as being:-

Touring chassis	£625
Sports Chassis	£625
Two-seater Sports	£695
3-seater cloverleaf	£695
4-seater	£720

| Super-Sports | £725 |
| 4-seater all-weather | £825 |

In December 1923 there had been mention of a coupé to order and 2 — 3 months' delivery on all models. Strangely, perhaps, no saloon body was listed, despite which at least four saloons are known to have been built. The Super-Sports was fitted with the 16-valve twin-overhead camshaft engine, the other models having the side-valve engines. Both the Sports and Super-Sports made use of the shorter wheelbase (8ft.0ins) chassis. Abingdon Road had no coachwork facilities so all bodies had to be made elsewhere and the variety of choice in those days being wide one would say that virtually no two Astons were identical, owners being allowed a fair degree of latitude to incorporate their personal whims and fancies.

Of the 1924 production cars the first (Car No. 1924) was in fact fitted with a saloon body (XP 5125). The owner of Car No. 1925 (Registered No. PD 8111) was Mr P.R. Callard, of Callard & Bowser, and he was quick to sing the car's praises in the columns of the motoring press, concluding his string of superlatives by remarking ". . . . . No amount of real hard driving seems to disturb it in any way, no trace of wear being apparent. Not a single nut on the car has worked loose, although driven hard over bad roads at times. In fact, it is, in my opinion, in a class by itself, and British." He had a word of praise too for both the Works and the London agents (G.L. Francis & Co.) of whom he said, ". . . . . nothing is too much trouble, and the car can be taken away after a job is done with the secure feeling that it is O.K., without having to investigate personally the work that has been put in . . . . ." Callard was an experienced motorist, having owned, so he claimed, some 35 motor cars prior to his purchase of the Aston-Martin.

Car No. 1928 (registered number DM 2986) was delivered new to R.F. Summers, then a Cambridge undergraduate, who drove it with a fair degree of success at times in a wide variety of competitions ranging from Brooklands events to sand-racing at Skegness and sprints such as Shelsley Walsh and Kop. Car No. 1929 was supplied to H.S. Eaton and unwittingly earned itself and its driver much commendation when it ran as a substitute in the 200-Miles Race and put up a race average of 79·55mph, achieving 12th place when running in 'touring' condition though naturally stripped of wings, lamps, hood and screen. Car No. 1934, a side-valver, was supplied new to Capt. G.E.T. Eyston whose exploits with the Aston racing cars had already gained him many successes. This car was fitted with a lightweight touring body by Compton & Hermon, of Hersham, Walton-on-Thames; somehow this body, though doubtless built to accord with Eyston's ideas, just failed to present a really homogeneous appearance. Registered XR 3941 Eyston competed with it when virtually brand new from the body shops at the Skegness sand races in June 1924, when *The Light Car & Cyclecar's* reporter referred to it as 'Eyston's new Aston-Martin'. This car is reputed to have been fitted with a 2-ohc engine for the 1925 200-Miles Race. Eyston bought the long-chassis track car back from R.C. Morgan after it had been repaired at the Works following Morgan's unhappy climb at South Harting. Morgan had acquired the car from McCulloch via Gordon Offord.

E.R. Hall had already had considerable experience with Astons, notably with 'Bunny' with which he had chalked up an impressive list of successes at sprints and races, and both he and his friend Noel Beardsell, who had campaigned a Super-Sports Hodgson, that rare Yorkshire sports car, also became private owners of Aston-Martins, side-valvers in each case. Beardsell and Hall entered these privately owned touring cars as well as, in Hall's case 'Bunny' or one of the other Works Astons, and in Beardsell's case, his Hodgson, at many such sprint events.

"New" names featured as Aston-Martin drivers in the 1924 season, including those of H.S. Eaton, Victor Gillow (who drove a twin overhead camshaft model described as being "Aluminium with red wheels" in the programme, that G.E.T. Eyston had entered for the 17th 90mph Long Handicap at the JCC Members Meeting at Brooklands on 3 May), Miss Lister, whose car was on occasions driven by one "J. Waters", better known to a later generation of film and television addicts as Jack Warner, R.H.McBean, A.A. Pollard and R.F. Summers. The regulars, Gallop, Morgan, Eyston and Hall featured too, of course, in the season's racing.

In the Whitsun Long Handicap on 9 June Morgan had entered a long-tailed track car with twin overhead camshaft engine. Within the week he was to make a meteoric, but alas unsuccessful, climb of South Harting. Of this climb the *Light Car & Cyclecar* wrote ".....and a climax was reached when R.C. Morgan in a new Aston-Martin electrified the crowd on the lower slopes, only to come to grief higher up, when he was within measurable distance of making the most sensational ascent that has ever been witnessed at a hill-climb....." Morgan had been persuaded by Kaye Don to enter the long-chassis car for this event, Don being under the mistaken impression that the straighter of the two optional courses was to be used. With the locked back axle on this car, it was difficult to control, with the unhappy results recorded.

At the Essex MC's hill-climb at Kop, held in bleak weather with a biting north-west wind on 29 March, Astons were out in force, Morgan, Summers and Hall, the latter with 'Razorblade', all competing. Morgan was driving the ex-Robertson all-weather car No. 1912 at this Kop event. Noel Beardsell had his touring Aston out for the Aston Clinton event in May, taking 4th place in the class for touring cars up to 3000cc. June found the Astons ever more active, with Capt. J.C. Douglas pulling off a third in one class and a second in another at the Blackpool Speed Trials, Eaton, Eyston and Summers active at the Skegness sand races, to say nothing of the South Harting event already referred to.

The intrepid Miss Pink was again driving an Aston at the Shelsley Walsh meeting on 12 July, at which event Summers, Beardsell and Hall also had their Astons out, Hall driving not only his own tourer but 'Bunny' as well, in different classes. *The Light Car & Cyclecar's* reporter at the event commented that Hall had brought his Aston-Martin down on a trailer constructed largely of Ford parts and towed behind a vast and imposing 1908 45hp Renault which he was reputed to have bought for a little over £30. Whether it was 'Bunny' or his personal side-valver that was brought to the meeting in this way is not recorded, however.

Meanwhile.....''back at the Works'' much of interest was taking place. In May 1924 there joined the Bamford & Martin Company a charming and outstandingly tall young man by the name of John Roby Benson, son of Lord Charnwood. An old Etonian and having but recently left King's College, London, and Oxford, young Benson was anxious to obtain a footing in motor engineering with a congenial Company whose outlook and interest in sporting machinery matched his own, and having some family capital to invest in such a project, the necessary negotiations were made with Lionel Martin. Benson's initial salary on joining Bamford & Martin was a princely £4 per week but as he had private means this was perhaps less niggardly than it would appear! Years later he liked to recount the tale that shortly after joining the little band at 53 Abingdon Road and being clearly regarded with some suspicion by those of greater practical experience he was faced with a current problem that was then besetting the works.....an 'epidemic' of chassis fractures. Put on his mettle by this challenge, Benson solved the problem characteristically. ''I realised that there was a stress concentration at that point (near the forward rear spring mounting) and *weakened* the frame at that point by drilling a hole. It then 'gave' slightly instead of fracturing and we had no further problem,'' he records.

Benson was to become on very friendly, almost filial, terms with Lionel and Katherine Martin, as had 'Bertie' Kensington Moir in earlier days, but later events were to cast deep shadows on this happy relationship. Benson was keen to design a new engine for the Aston-Martin and the 1924 200-Miles Race seemed to offer a suitable target for a new effort from the racing department. The new racer was to be powered by Benson's new twin overhead camshaft 8-valve design of engine, a unit which still retained the old Robb-designed bottom half and was also to make use of a machined Strasbourg block, the whole thing being what Benson himself described as "something of a bodge-up". The car itself had the basis of a standard long-chassis frame on which was built an all-aluminium streamlined racing body with cowled radiator and full undershielding. A serious misfortune compounded of exuberance and misunderstanding unfortunately put the car out of the running even before the race itself, for it was being towed back, newly bodied, from the coachbuilders to Abingdon Road, minus engine and therefore very light at the front. It is said that Lionel Martin, perhaps forgetting that the racer was in tow, couldn't resist an impromptu race with another car, and Benson, at the wheel of the racer, could only attempt to follow "on the string" as his car became less controllable as speed rose. The whole incident came to a sudden and violent end when the car wrapped itself round a lorry.

Spectacular crashes seem to loom rather large in the Aston milieu that year, for Capt. Douglas in Car No. 1920, his long-chassis tourer, managed an even more spectacular one when returning with his wife from a dinner visit to the Mr Greenall who had bought the first production fwb car, No. 1919. He succeeded in clouting a road bollard on an 'island' with such force that the crankcase was shattered (the full force of the blow fell on the starting handle), the crankshaft concertina-ed, the rear axle bent into a curve and the dumb-irons had to be prised apart to release the car from the entangled street furniture! However, the car was towed back to 53 Abingdon Road and repaired and is, perhaps surprisingly, but happily, still extant, though latterly much changed in appearance. Capt. Douglas recovered from the effects of this smash and had the car back after its repair.....and continued to race Aston-Martins. Douglas's wife was very badly scarred on the face in this accident, the screen (not of safety glass) being shattered.

Of passing interest is the Birkin-Comery which appeared in 1924, this sports/racing car having a 2-litre engine designed by H.R.S. ('Tim') Birkin, later to be so famously associated with Bentley, Alfa-Romeo and Maserati racing cars, and W. Comery. This engine was fitted in an Aston-Martin chassis and called the Birkin-Comery and appeared at a number of events in the 1924 season, putting up a time of 26·4 secs in the 1-Kilometre Herne Bay Speed Trials and also appearing at the Skegness Sand Races in June.

The specially prepared 200-Miles racer having crashed shortly before the race, as recounted above, H.S. Eaton was prevailed upon to enter his touring side-valver as a hasty substitute. This car's average of 79·55mph overall was a most creditable performance and one to which Lionel Martin frequently referred later, as the following quotation from a letter of 5 March 1925 to a prospective client shows — "....last year in the 200-Miles race a private owner with a standard touring car finished at an average of 79·5....."

George Eyston had crashed his Aston racer during the Boulogne Week races and had been given a 'lift' back to the pits by Robert Morgan whose well-known 'Green Pea' with side-valve engine then retired, having suffered from persistent magneto maladies. Eaton with his game side-valve tourer had been forced to retire when leading the field in this event on account of running out of petrol.

October was to bring the most shattering crash to date in the Aston-Martin fortunes, for on the 19th of the month Count 'Lou' Zborowski was killed while driving for Mercedes in the Italian Grand Prix at Monza. With his tragic death was lost a great sportsman, a great driver, a great personal friend of Lionel and Katherine Martin and a much-needed financial backer of the brave little Kensington firm for whom serious shortage of money was again looming even before the sad accident to Zborowski. The Count had always been of superstitious disposition and indeed it would almost seem as if his ill-omened death was to cast a spell of misfortune on the affairs of Aston-Martin for it is from this time that, however inevitable the firm's ultimate demise must seem when looked at in the cold unromatic realism of hindsight, things from then on began increasingly to go awry in the affairs of the Company.

But for Lionel Martin himself the omens of ill-fortune had loomed menacingly even earlier in that eventful year. Ever since the inception of his dream to make the ideal sporting light car the project had been almost entirely financed out of his own pocket. Zborowski, it is true, had contributed some £10,000 at the time of the twin-overhead camshaft racing cars project, but by the summer of 1924 Bamford & Martin were in Martin's debt to the tune of some £31,000 and Martin's financial resources were stretched to the limit. Some indication of this may be gleaned from the fact that when R.C. Morgan had repairs done to his 2-ohc track car after the debacle at South Harting, Martin, in forwarding the account for some £65, sent a covering letter dated 2 July 1924 which I quote in full:-

"Dear Mr Morgan,
Your long racer will be ready to-morrow morning
first thing. You already have the invoice for the
work, and as the amount is such a large one, and
we, as you know, are running on our private
means, I should be very much obliged if you
would let us have your cheque when you collect
your car.

Yours faithfully,
Lionel Martin"

If the whole project were not to slide into ignominious oblivion, despite the many stresses that had already come its way, new money must be found, and found quickly. John Benson, who had joined the Company in May of that year, was perhaps the instigator and certainly the instrument of the idea that Martin should approach his mother, Lady Charnwood. Benson's enthusiasm for the work he was engaged in for Aston-Martin was obvious and he and Mr and Mrs Martin were at that time on very friendly terms. Lady Charnwood was approached and at first agreed to put up £5,000 if others would put up £35,000. The "others" in question appeared difficult to find so a second approach was made to Lady Charnwood who then agreed to put up £10,000 on first debenture and to acquire the assets of the old Company.

Accordingly in July 1924 a new Company was formed with Lionel Martin, Katherine Martin, George Eustace Ridley Shield and John Roby Benson as Directors. The sizeable debt outstanding to Lionel Martin was cancelled on his receipt of £22,350-worth of shares in the new Company and he was to receive a salary of £700 per annum. John Benson, now with a seat on the Board, received 7,500 shares in the new Company and his salary was raised to £5 per week. Shortly afterwards Martin suggested further economies and proposed a voluntary cut in his own salary to £600 per annum.

So on this revitalised but hardly rosy basis 1924 gave way to 1925. The first production car of the year was unique in being the only full Grand Prix Replica sold to an ' outside' client. This was Car No. 1950 which was sold to a M. Riva, a Swiss gentleman, and the car was never registered in this country. Car No. 1952, a standard long-chassis side-valve tourer registered XY 5471 was supplied to W.L. Booty who raced it frequently at Brooklands and elsewhere. Car No. 1953 was one of the rare saloons but did not retain this body for long as it soon appeared with an open tourer body and rather ugly cycle wings and was raced by a Mr Randall. This car was registered RO99.

In the field of competition many of the old 'regulars' were still campaigning their Aston-Martins, including Capt. Douglas who was often to be seen at the wheel of 'Razorblade', having recovered from his nasty smash in his own side-valver FY 6193. H.S. Eaton and R.H. McBean were also active as was R.C. Morgan with 'Green Pea', though by now this car had exchanged its side-valve Aston engine for a Hooker-Thomas engine obtained from the great J.G. Parry Thomas, who was a friend of Morgan's. This unusual engine was a long-stroke four-cylinder with a single overhead camshaft and incorporated leaf valve springs as on Thomas's Leyland Eights. 'Green Pea' now had an even better performance than it had so ably shown in tuned side-valve form. It was re-registered as PE 2516 on 5 May 1925 and named a 'Thomas Special'. As such it had been entered for the GP de l'Ouverture at Montlhéry to be run on 17 May. (Incidentally, the car was run with stub exhausts in this event, but retired with valve trouble). The race proved to be yet another victory for the 1½-litre Talbots with a spectacular finish when Duller crossed the line first, to be followed by Conelli with his car upside-down (!) and Segrave in 3rd position. Mrs Marion Morgan, who was present with her future husband at this event, recalled vividly that Conelli's head appeared to be taking the whole weight of the car before the car did a cartwheel and flung Conelli out. She recalled that poor Conelli seemed to bounce like 'a rag doll', yet he was able to walk, with help, a few minutes later. Capt. Alastair Miller, well-known at Brooklands for his exploits with a variety of cars, was also an Aston-Martin entrant and driver in this event with the ex-Zborowski GP car, still painted white, Zborowski's colour. This Aston was the one registered as XP 3037 in September 1923 and had later been crashed in France and brought back to Higham where it had been fitted with a new chassis and then given new bodywork by Bligh's. Sidney Maslin, who was one of Zborowski's mechanics at the time, actually worked on the rebuild of this car at Higham and recalled to the author that they had problems in mating up the propshaft splines, hence the unusual angle of the rear spring shackles that has been a feature of this car since and identifies the car as XP 3037.

At Shelsley Walsh Miss Pink again drove AM 270 and R.F. Summers drove his side-valver (Car No. 1928); he had a new racing body in mottled aluminium with an elegantly pointed tail built for this car by Compton & Hermon.

Capt. G.E.T. Eyston, staunch supporter of the make, was at this time turning his attention to speedboat racing and had a racing boat built for him by The Walton Launch Co. This was powered by a 16-valve twin ohc Aston-Martin engine of the type used in the Strasbourg cars of 1922. This boat was named "Miss Olga" and it, together with another boat again built by The Walton Launch Co., and named "Pampero" took part in the Eliminating Trials for The Duke of York's Trophy at Mortlake in June 1925. "Pampero" too was Aston-Martin engined, but her engine was one of the new 8-valve twin ohc units designed by Benson. Count Johnston-Noad also had his Aston-Martin-engined "Miss Betty" which like Eyston's "Miss Olga" had the Strasbourg pattern engine. Camper & Nicholson had built "Miss Betty's" hull. Out of the 9 starters, "Miss Betty" finished 3rd, "Miss Olga" was 6th and the unfortunate "Pampero" of C.W. Burnard capsized while making a tight turn, her Benson-designed engine filling with Thames mud. Much to its detriment an attempt was made to re-start it when the boat was recovered, an exercise which did it no good whatever.

The Duke of York's Trophy was run off on two days in June. On Thursday 18 June "Miss Betty" was second at 32.0 knots and "Miss Olga" 5th at 28.6 knots while on the following day "Miss Olga" managed a 2nd place at 28.6 knots but she was one of only two finishers! All this Aston-Martin activity in a strange element was much to the pleasure and interest of Lionel Martin who spent much time at the trials of both "Miss Olga" and "Miss Betty" and was present at the running off of the Trophy itself. He and Count Johnston-Noad and the representatives of Camper & Nicholson were in frequent riverside discussion at times when tests, modifications and race tactics were being worked out.

Despite so much activity in this and the motor racing field and the worry and stress of keeping the Company's head above water Lionel Martin found time to answer with the greatest kindness and consideration, letters from potential customers and, indeed, anyone with a genuine interest in the Aston-Martin project. As an example of his usual impeccable good manners in matters of this kind I quote from two letters written in June and August 1925 respectively, to F.E. Ellis, at that time quite unknown to Martin, but, of course, the selfsame F.E. Ellis who was later to become a friend of Lionel and Mrs Martin and to do so much to keep alive an interest in the Bamford & Martin Astons.'

"(Dated) 2/vi/25.

> *Dear Mr Ellis,*
> *Please excuse the delay in acknowledging*
> *your kind letter and photograph, the holidays*

and the rush preceding them were too much for
me! Thank you very much indeed for the
photograph. I think it shows the model to far
greater advantage than that of the one with the
body on — the photographs deceive everyone —
even people who know the cars very well; they all
think it is a 'real' car.....As I am sure you are
an Aston-Martin enthusiast I am sure you will be
glad to know that we had a win at Brooklands
yesterday — the single-seater with a standard
side-valve engine in.'

> *Again thanking you,*
> *Yours truly,*

> *Lionel Martin* ''

and ''*(dated) 26/viii/25.*

Dear Mr Ellis,
> *Very many thanks for your letter and*
the photograph of the model and your good self,
also the cutting of Zborowski in Spain, which I
return.....
> *.....Cook's Vauxhall has not been*
tried since the new body was fitted; it is supposed
to be ready to-day, as a matter of fact.
> *His Aston-Martin is a long-chassis and*
the body is like that of the Vauxhall except for
the undershield, which is 'square', and the whole
thing is made of fabric. She will really be
finished on Monday, she had no engine in when
the photograph was taken.....''

The model referred to was a model made by Ellis, presumably of an Aston-Martin, though alas, the whole of the letter from which this quotation was taken does not appear to have survived, so this is but conjecture on the author's part. However, one could scarcely believe otherwise in view of what is quoted above. That Lionel Martin should have gone to such trouble in answering in this way at a time when Aston-Martin affairs were not only hectic but also not without an element of stress is indeed a credit to his kindliness and good manners that so often drew favourable comment from others.

Lionel Martin always remained faithful to his cycling interest too, and even at this same hectic period in his affairs he found time to act as one of the judges for the Bath Road's Open Tricycle Scratch "50" held on 21 June 1925, and *The Bath Road News* in writing of Martin at this time recalls "Lionel Martin was ever polite. Some of you will recollect the occasion of a certain tandem attempt (not of our Club) at which Lionel was helping. The riders, two most offensive fellows, had had bad luck. They described their trouble to Mr Martin. 'Yus, we wos just coming rahnd the blinkin' corner when all of a suddint the blarsted back tyre bust and I sey Dash it, I sey.' 'Did you *really*?' says Martin, in his best 'Varsity voice'.

It is said that Porter, later of Boon & Porter, at one time applied to Lionel Martin for a job involving test driving, and that Martin took him out in his own Aston-Martin in order to test Porter's suitability for the job. At the conclusion of the run Porter asked Martin how he had done. Martin replied, "Well, Mr Porter, you have one inestimable advantage." Porter's spirits took an upward turn. "You'll never meet another chap who drives like Mr Porter!" Martin continued.....and Porter didn't get the job!

The mention of Cook's Aston-Martin in the letter to Ellis refers, of course, to the special long-chassis racer, Car No. 1961, built with the 1925 JCC 200-Miles Race in mind, for Humphrey Cook to drive. The race was to take place on September 26 and early entries gave every hope of a fine race, with the Darracqs (and Segrave in particular) as favourites. During practice the new Aston-Martin racer wore the Registration No. YL 3717 and carried the number 4 in the race itself. It had been intended that this new racer should be fitted with John Benson's revised version of the 8-valve twin-cam engine, a design that would at last have done away with the old Robb-designed bottom end with its inherent troubles, but alas, this engine could not be made ready in time and it was with one of the 16-valve 2-ohc engines that it came to the line. Lionel Martin, writing many years later to (the late) F.E. Ellis, remarked of the engine fitted in Cook's car; "The only block we had had been accidentally over bored and would have come outside 1500cc with a normal crankshaft, so a different shaft, giving shorter stroke, was designed for and fitted to this engine." Other Aston-Martin participants were Eyston, H.S. Eaton (again with his 'touring' side-valver that had acquitted itself so nobly the previous year), and R.C. Morgan's car, now with Hooker-Thomas engine and sporting a cowled radiator. Halford had his 'A.M.-Halford', later to be further modified and termed the Halford Special. This car consisted of a standard Aston-Martin chassis but was fitted with Halford's own highly sophisticated 6-cylinder 2-ohc engine. In its early form, as in this event, it still carried a normal Aston-Martin radiator, and without looking under the bonnet there was little to distinguish it from a normal Aston.

Alas for any hopes for the new racer, which had not shone in practice and had exhibited considerable front wheel bounce when the brakes were applied, for it was out of the race on the very first lap, going out of control and crashing, pinning Cook and his mechanic beneath the car. Cook's injuries were slight but his mechanic had to be taken to hospital. Eyston retired with a run big-end, Morgan likewise with carburettor trouble, and Eaton was flagged off after completing 41 laps. Halford with the AM — Halford fared slightly better, coming in 4th in the 1½-litre class but 6th in the general classification.

With the 200-Miles Race over for another season and alas, little kudos for Aston-Martin in the results, all efforts were now concentrated on the firm's appearance at Olympia for the Motor Show. Surprisingly, perhaps, this 1925 Show was the first at which Aston-Martin had a stand — No. 70 — and it was also destined to be the last, under the Bamford & Martin banner at any rate. The *Motor Trader* in its descriptive paragraph remarks, "In specification the Aston-Martin follows the most advanced lines for fast touring, only a slight modification being necessary to place it well inside the fastest class of 1500cc." while *The Garage & Motor Agent* for 17 October 1925 comments "A welcome newcomer to Olympia was the Aston-Martin, which has been a centre of admiration from its own particular public all the week....." In a feature article entitled "Some Mechanical Matters at Olympia" the same journal remarked: ".....The valve controversy has reached an interesting stage. Overheads are very much on the increase this year, and this method of construction has, for the average user, an advantage with which it is not always credited, namely, that tappet adjustment is apt to be a more convenient job than it is in the case of a side-valve engine. In conjunction with a detachable head, it is in fact a question whether or not the ohv engine is not more easily looked after than a s.v. On the other hand, while the greater efficiency of the overhead is commonly taken for granted, *it is significant that such an experienced constructor as Mr Lionel Martin should stick to side-valves for the Aston-Martin standard models*....." (the italics are the author's). Perhaps the commentator hadn't appreciated that the sv Astons still retained a fixed-head? Be that as it may, it is an interesting comment.

What Aston-Martin had on display was a boat-decked 3/4-seater with a most elegant single-door body finished in pale yellow with brown wings, a standard tourer finished in two-tone red, and the Benson 8-valve 2-ohc engine that should have been ready for Cook's 200-Miles racer, this engine being polished and mounted as a centre-piece on the stand. *The Autocar* quotes the boat-decked sports model at £825 and in its abbreviated specification quotes a chassis price of £625 with the standard tourer at £725.

However, being "a centre of admiration" for the week of the Show was not enough to stave off what had by now become almost inevitable. Matters that were only to come to light a year later reveal that these last months of activity, suspense and disappointments at 53 Abingdon Road must indeed have imposed severe strains upon the personal relationships of many concerned, and one senses that an atmosphere of tension and mistrust clouded these last few months of the firm's existence.

CHAPTER SIX

Even while the excitement of the Motor Show was still a major topic in the motoring press nemesis came to 53 Abingdon Road in the form of the appointment of the Receiver, Mr Arthur Whale, on 11 November 1925. Thereafter events moved swiftly and any last shreds of hope for the survival of the brave little firm must have rapidly evaporated. For Lionel Martin in particular this must have been a bitter blow, for his services were dispensed with and on 13 November, only two days after the appointment of the Receiver, he left the Works for the last time, his idealistic dream shattered and a considerable part of his personal fortune gone beyond any reasonable hope of recovery.

To learn more of this unfortunate period it is perhaps best to move forward by a year to discover what was revealed in the outcome of an even more unfortunate episode — unfortunate in that it was so obviously the result of the seriously strained personal relationships that the final months of the Company's existence, with all their frustrations, uncertainties and slender hopes buoyed up by so much fragile optimism had brought about. If the collapse of the Company was a shattering blow to Lionel Martin himself, as indeed it was, there is no doubt that it was a disaster, too, in the eyes of young John Benson. Even if nothing whatever could be rescued from the ashes of the old firm neither he nor his family had so much financially at stake as had Lionel Martin, but Benson was nothing if not enthusiastic over the new engine that he, as Chief Engineer, had developed and which up to then, through a series of misfortunes, had never really had the opportunity to prove itself. Now, with the Receiver called in and only bleak prospects at best for the future of his design and his aspirations, he must have felt bitterly disappointed at the way things had turned out so soon after he had first become associated with the Aston-Martin project. Perhaps this understandably black mood bred indiscretion; perhaps too this sorry turn of events triggered minor grievances into major ones and doubts and misgivings into suspicions and accusations. Whatever the reasons that lay behind the events Benson did make unfortunate and critical remarks in the hearing of others and these remarks reached Martin's ears.

Perhaps at a less stressful time in the earlier relationship between John Benson and Mr and Mrs Martin such remarks would have been laughed off good-naturedly but coming when they did just when Martin had been ignominiously 'dismissed' by the Receiver and had seen his dream of the fortunes of the Aston-Martin crumble about him, there was little chance that such remarks would be ignored or dismissed lightly, especially so when one realises that Martin was always quick — some might say too quick — to involve the processes of law when he felt his position or his opinions to be seriously challenged. One has only to refer to his unsuccessful appeal against sentence for motoring offences mentioned in Chapter II or to his attempt (again unsuccessful) to sue a leading Bournemouth hotel which he alleged had failed in its statutory obligations when dealing with his wife's requests.

Benson is alleged to have said (a) that Martin had been party to a conspiracy with Addis (the Works Foreman) to remove the Aston-Martin working drawings without Benson's knowledge or consent; (b) that Martin did not manage the Company well; (c) that Martin, in conjunction with Addis, removed spare parts which, the Company being in the Receiver's hands, he had no right to do; (d) that Martin had stolen some tyres; and (e) that the Ledgers of the Company were in a disgraceful state.

Martin sued for damages for alleged slander and the case came before the court in October 1926, the plaintiff (Lionel Martin) being represented by Mr Norman Birkett, KC and Mr John W. Morris. The defendant, John Benson, was represented by Sir Leslie Scott, KC and Mr Hugh Beazley. The words complained of were said to have been uttered by the defendant on three different occasions and to three separate persons in November 1925, and to impute dishonesty to the plaintiff.

Among the many witnesses called were J.G. Parry Thomas, the famous designer and racing motorist, Hugh P. McConnell, the Brooklands Scrutineer, Capt. J.C. Douglas, motoring correspondent and racing motorist, and Mr and Mrs Greenall who were early owners of an Aston-Martin and friends of the Martins. The case lasted for a week and the court was crowded on most days, according to *The Times*.

Giving evidence, Benson said that after the Company went into the Receiver's hands in November 1925 he came to distrust both Lionel and Katherine Martin. He also alleged that Addis, the Works Foreman, had been stealing extensively from the Works and that he (Benson) had never trusted

110

him and did not think much of him as Works Manager. He also stated that he suspected Addis of deliberately attempting to wreck his (Benson's) engine by putting cast-iron bolts in it, and that this attempt on Addis's part was done with Martin's knowledge or connivance. Addis, who was paid a salary of £11 per week at the time his engagement with the Company ended when the Receiver took over, had emigrated to New Zealand in December 1925. Both Martin and Benson knew of his intention to do so.

Cross-examined by Sir Leslie Scott, Martin was asked, "Did you help him to go?". "Not in any sense", Martin replied emphatically. Questioned further by Sir Leslie Scott as to what his reactions would be if the allegations were true, Martin replied that if they were true he would be unable to appear in public again.

In giving his evidence Benson had also referred to Katherine Martin in somewhat unapproving terms. He had said that she was frequently given to making statements of a wildly inaccurate nature and that she was vindictive, though not to him personally. To assess the validity or otherwise of Benson's criticism of Katherine Martin perhaps it would be as well to enlarge a little on the reactions that this undoubtedly strong-minded lady inspired in others.

For one thing she was universally known among her friends and acquaintances (though presumably not, of course, to her face) as 'Calamity Kate'. It is said that the entire personnel at the Works lived in dread of her. Alas, the author has no more than hearsay to go on with regard to those who worked at 53 Abingdon Road, but others have confirmed the widespread application of this soubriquet. Mrs Kensington Moir, talking to the author over fifty years later, referred to her as 'a diabolical woman — nobody liked her.' Certainly there was no love lost between Mrs Moir and Mrs Martin at the time Kensington Moir was in Martin's employ and Mrs Moir recalls that Mrs Martin did her best to break the engagement of 'Bertie' Kensington Moir and his then fiancée and that Mrs Martin was pointedly not invited to the Moir wedding in 1923. Mrs Moir describes Lionel Martin, by contrast, as 'a dear old thing'.

Perhaps the opinions of one who knew Katherine Martin and remained within her circle of friends for a much longer period may serve in some way to give a broader view. Mrs A.G. Gripper who, with her husband, was much concerned in competitive motor sport in the 1920s and 1930s, says of Katherine Martin: "To say she was a forceful character is putting it mildly! 'Bossy' would be better! Although many people fell out with her, for some reason she and I remained good friends till she died, possibly because I

111

happen to be even-tempered. She must have driven Lionel Martin nearly mad at times. He was nearly always one of the stewards at the Brooklands race meetings and other trials, and a stickler for rules being carried out. Kate, on the other hand, completely disregarded them, and I have seen her walk right across the starting paddock even after the warning siren had gone!'' And on matters less directly concerned with motoring she continues; ''Kate, I feel sure, could have seen any man under the table and all the difference to her was a slightly 'glassy' look in the eyes. She was always ready to help anyone in trouble, and I can think of several people who have reason to be grateful to her, when they were without a home and she took them in until things improved for them; but she still liked to be boss! So, you can see, she was a bit of a mixed person, and if one did fall out with her, her tongue could be somewhat biting about them, and others.''

So, it would seem that Benson's accusation of vindictiveness was not without foundation. She was one of those vivid personalities for whom there are no 'greys', only 'blacks' or 'whites' — she was either totally against or totally in favour, opinions probably attributable to feminine instinct rather than to a process of reasoning, but nevertheless not uncommon in those of a similar nature. But to revert to the slander case in the King's Bench Division under Mr Justice McCardie.

Giving evidence, Martin strongly denied that he had either personally prevented, or given any instructions that any other person was to prevent, Benson from knowing that the Aston-Martin working drawings had been removed from the premises. Martin stated that they had been removed to his (and the Company's) solicitors so that they could be seen by any persons interested in the rescue of the Company and the possible resumption of production. He also vigorously denied that he had in any way been party with Addis or any other person to the placing of cast-iron bolts in the Benson engine. During the hearing a certain amount of 'cloak and dagger' explanations and counter-explanations relating to the alleged removal by Martin and Addis of a box of spare parts were aired, and the Works' storekeeper and certain other employees were called to give evidence, and it was in relation to these activities that Benson, when questioned himself, imputed ''wildly inaccurate statements'' to Mrs Martin. That Martin had expended some £31,000 of his own fortune on the Company up to mid-1924 was again said in evidence, and it also transpired that Mr and Mrs Greenall and Capt. Douglas had repeatedly expressed their sorrow and regret to Benson and to Martin that the whole situation should have been allowed to reach such a pass that the case was brought and that commonsense should have prevailed, but that Martin was adamant and eventually sued for

112

damages for alleged slander.

After an absence of four hours the jury returned with a verdict in favour of the plaintiff (Martin), awarding him ¼d damages on each of the seven counts, amounting to 1¾d in all. In answer to the seven questions put to them by Mr Justice McCardie, the jury found that the statements had been made and that the plea of justification failed. Mr Justice McCardie said that he had no hesitation in depriving Mr Martin of his costs, the jury having expressed their view of the case in the plainest manner, but later, on application by the plaintiff's counsel, he agreed that the question of costs should be reserved, and at the same time he released the jury from further service for five years.

This sad and unhappy washing of dirty linen in the courts was a matter of the deepest regret to John Benson, who, many years later as Lord Charnwood, spoke feelingly of his sorrow that the happy friendship that he had enjoyed with Lionel and Katherine Martin should have been so bitterly clouded in this way.

Meanwhile, what of the fortunes of the Company itself rather than of its leading personalities? Martin himself told of the talks which were held with representatives of Vauxhall Motors, the Bristol Aeroplane Co., and perhaps surprisingly, Donnet-Zedel, presumably with a view to one of these Companies taking over and perhaps even resuming production of the Aston-Martin cars, but all these talks proved fruitless, alas, and it was eventually the Charnwoods (Benson's parents) who purchased the goodwill and assets of the old Company and approached the small Birmingham firm of Renwick and Bertelli with a view to forming some sort of amalgamation. As a result the firm of Aston Martin Motors Ltd., was incorporated on 12 October 1926 and a new chapter in the chequered history of the make was about to begin.

Martin, of course, had his mining and quarrying interests to attend to and it was to these that he gave of his time and efforts extensively, so that he virtually retired from the motoring scene during 1926 and 1927. His son John, then about to go to his public school, recalls that his father was never, within his hearing at any rate, openly bitter or critical of the way that affairs had turned out, though the fact that he felt this sad turn of events deeply was for a long time apparent in ways other than the tangible results of this downward turn in the family's personal fortunes, among which the fact that he himself could not follow in his father's footsteps to Eton was but one manifestation.

113

One may perhaps gauge something of Lionel's reactions to this change in the tide of events by a remark made in a letter dated 10 August 1928 to (the late) F.E. Ellis, in which Martin remarks: "I am afraid I am no longer running an Aston-Martin as I have no wish to give the new company an advertisement; I have not heard of their producing anything for sale yet, and they certainly have not distinguished themselves in competition....."

However, it is not really surprising, Martin having motoring and motor competition so much at heart, that he was quick to realise and to assess the qualities of another newly introduced small car which if not built to quite the same exacting standards as the original Aston-Martins was to be the precursor of a long line of successful competition cars. Martin had always pinned his faith in the high-efficiency small car, and the recently introduced Riley Nine quickly caught his attention. In the same letter to Ellis he goes on to say: ".....I like the new Riley very much indeed, it is a willing little beast and can exceed 70mph on the road, doing a Brooklands lap at 69·6 as a saloon with all on; few cars will do this.....". Indeed, at this period he had a Riley Nine saloon and followed it with an open model which Katherine Martin raced at Brooklands events and elsewhere about this time (1928).

In that same year Martin was elected a member of the British Racing Drivers Club (BRDC) and Katherine Martin was a member of the Women's Automobile and Sports Association (W.A.S.A.) and both were to become increasingly active in the world of motor competition, Lionel chiefly on the administrative side and Katherine taking part in a number of relatively minor events such as those held by the BARC at an evening meeting on 21 June 1928 when they staged a Ladies Race in which she competed with the black Riley Nine. Ironically, one of her rivals in this event was Miss H.M. Lister, driving the old Bamford & Martin Aston that she (Miss Lister) and Waters had driven in the palmy days of the old firm. Indeed a number of the earlier Aston-Martins continued to be active in competition in private hands after the demise of the old firm. These appeared mostly in minor events, though Capt. G.E.T. Eyston drove his Aston, fitted with a supercharged Anzani engine, in the 1926 British Grand Prix at Brooklands.

By late 1929 the Rileys had given place to a new M.G., the 18/80 model, and in a letter to Ellis dated 1 November 1929 Martin remarks: "I am now using myself an M.G. 6-cyl., with which I am very pleased." Whether this was an example of the new and much improved Mk.II version introduced at the 1919 Show or one of the earlier Mk.Is he doesn't make clear but the latter seems more likely unless Lionel had pulled some pretty weighty strings. At any rate it carried a fabric saloon body (a choice perhaps influenced by the Riley Monaco

69.   Summers at Shelsley Walsh again in 1925

70.   Capt. G.E.T. Eyston replenishing the tank of his 2-ohc
GP car, while Lionel Martin may be seen in waistcoat and
shirtsleeves bending down behind the pit counter, and the
figure in goggles and helmet is J.G. Parry Thomas

71. Internals: crankshaft and
con-rods from side-valve
engine No. 1924

72. Car No. 1920 (FY 6193) after Capt. Douglas' argument with a road bollard, 1924

73. 'Green Pea' at Brooklands immediately prior to the 200-Miles Race, 1925, with the Hooker-Thomas engine fitted. R.C. Morgan and Marion Morgan pose suitably

74. Lionel Martin is beside Miss W. Pink, the driver, and an energetic passenger 'occupies' the rear seat as Miss Pink takes AM 270 up Shelsley in 1923

75. Miss Pink again; she is seen here with Car No. 1939, registered XT 4102 which had started life as one of the rare saloons

76. A number of private competitors continued to use the pre-Bertelli Astons in competition after the Receiver had taken over at Abingdon Road. Here in the line up for the start of the JCC 1500cc Short Handicap at Brooklands on 30 April 1927 are portrayed Car No. 1952, XY 5471, driven by W.L. Booty, and 4th from right the 2-ohc car of Capt. Basil Eyston

77. Behind the leading Salmson (No. 48) is Car No. 1953, registered RO 99 being raced by Randall in the JCC High Speed Trial of 18 June 1927. Like XT 4102 this car too started life as a saloon

78.   Portrayed within this Fiat 501 at the same JCC High Speed Trial is F.T. Bidlake engaged in timekeeping. Formerly a great racing cyclist, Bidlake was very greatly admired by Lionel Martin

79. Capt. Ward's old car, with Jarvis 2-seater body, is here being taken through a watersplash by A.G. Gripper, later a noted Frazer Nash exponent, whose wife, a friend of the Martins, was also an accomplished racing and trials driver

80. This semi-overhead view of a long-chassis tourer, registered CX 6595, reveals the pleasing lines of the majority of these cars. It was taken on Wrynose Pass and portrays either Eddy Hall's or Noel Beardsell's personal car. Precise evidence as to its ownership is unreliable, but it is certainly a 1924 car

81. Martin in conversation
with Malcolm Campbell at
Brooklands, 1927

82. Clive Gallop in the driving seat with Lord Charnwood (John Benson) in the cloverleaf of a side-valve Aston-Martin portrayed in the 1950's

MODERN STREAMLINING.

A New Single-seater which Shows the Trend of Modern Design for High-speed Cars.

Two views of the new single-seater Aston-Martin racer, showing how the driver gets out of the car by lowering one side of the body and raising the lid. This car has been dubbed "The Oyster" at Brooklands, and it is probably the narrowest racing car at present in existence having the driver entirely within the streamline.

SEVERAL quite unusual features are to be found in the new 1,500 c.c. Aston-Martin single-seater, photographs of which appear on this page. In the first place, the springs and brake drums for the rear axle are placed very close to the bevel casing, only the driving shafts projecting on each side, and having at the end of them the wheels. There is no differential, and the rear wheels are quite close together, whereas the front wheels are the normal distance apart, giving the car what is known as a crab track.

The idea underlying the design was to keep everything as narrow as possible, in contradistinction to the theory which says that the true streamline form should be used. For this reason the chassis frame is arranged in a manner the reverse of usual. Ordinarily, the frame is inswept at the front; in this car it is inswept at the rear, the steering gear, pedals, etc., being, of course, mounted in the centre. The engine is the overhead-valve design with two camshafts which appeared for the last 200 Miles Race.

Even the body has some novel features; its width is only just sufficient for the driver, any air which enters through the radiator finds an outlet through a slot in the tail, and in order to avoid the large open cockpit of the ordinary car the whole top of the body near the driver is hinged and has to be opened to admit him. Once in the seat, one side of the body is raised, and the top dropped down and secured in position, only the driver's head being seen above the streamlining.

It is probable that this car will be very fast, its trials having proved quite satisfactory. Contrary to expectation, it is easy to hold and quite comfortable.

1925 LONDON MOTOR SHOW

ASTON-MARTIN. (70.)
Country of Origin: England.

BAMFORD AND MARTIN, LTD., 53, ABINGDON ROAD, KENSINGTON, W.8.

11 h.p. 4 cyls., 66.5×107 mm. (1,496 c.c.), tax £11, forced lub., Watford magneto, S.U. carb., 4-sp. separate gear box, plate cl., spiral bevel, ½-E. front and rear springs, 4 wheels braked, 710×90 mm. tyres on wire wheels, Lucas lighting and starting. Price: Chassis, £625; standard 4-seater, £725.

ALL enthusiastic British motorists, and quite a number of Continental automobilists also, know the Aston-Martin as one of the fastest and most roadworthy 1,500 c.c. touring cars obtainable. It is made in two types, the difference lying in the engine. On the touring car this has side valves, on the sports model—of which a finely made example is shown—an eight-valve twin overhead - camshaft 65×112 mm. engine

Speedy and graceful are the lines of the 11·9 h.p. Aston-Martin three-seater.

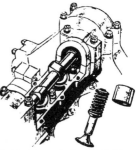

is fitted. These cars excel at speed work, and are admirable to handle. Two complete vehicles are exhibited, both on the touring chassis. One is a boat-shaped three-four-seater, painted pale yellow with brown wings. It has a single door, and over the tail is a detachable hatch cover which conceals a cockpit providing two occasional seats. The driving compartment has at the front a V-screen, and a hood is provided which can be detached completely, folded and housed in the tail. The car is priced at £825.

On the second car is a full four-seater body with a sunk well to give more leg room in the rear compartment. Two doors are provided; and the vehicle is most attractively finished in two shades of red. Both cars give an impression of speed in their racy lines

On the twin overhead camshaft Aston-Martin engine the valves are operated by sliding cups between the cams and valve stems.

83.   Drawing of the valve operation on the Benson-designed 8-valve 2-ohc engine

84.   'Palings', Kingston-on-Thames, to which the Martins moved early in 1932 and which remained their home until Lionel's death

85.   Lionel Martin (2nd from left) and Sir 'Algy' Guinness, RAC Chief Steward, at the 500-Miles Race, September 1932, talking to the driver of the C. Paul/J. Philip Riley at the pits

86. Lionel Martin, John Martin and Henry Gadsby with the Hillman 'Wizard' at the summit of the Stelvio, 1931

87. John Martin stands beside the Hillman on the rough descent from the Col du Parpaillon, 1931

88. The all-woman crew of the Hillman 'Wizard' prepare the car at 'Palings' for the 1933 Monte Carlo Rally

89.   Car and crew victorious;
they gained the John O'Groats
Ladies Award

90. Shelsley Squelch. Lionel Martin
(5th from left), Earl Howe (plus
umbrella), Leslie Wilson (6th from
left) and other celebrities pose in the
farmyard

91.   Kate and Lionel in the Wolseley
Hornet they drove in the 1932
International Alpine Trial . . .

92. . . . and with the Humber Twelve they drove in the following year's event, here portrayed before the event . . .

93.   . . . and at Nice during the Trial

94. Lionel smiles as he appears about to be swallowed by his much-liked BMW with special English drophead bodywork at Brooklands

95. The factory staff at 53
Abingdon Road form a background to one of the 1922
2-ohc racers. Jack Addis at the
wheel

with which Martin had been so delighted?) and this M.G. was followed by another 18/80, this time with a coachbuilt saloon body.

Two further quotations from this same letter to Ellis are not without interest. "Mrs Martin was hardly accurate when she told you I went to Manchester once a month; I used to, but now once a quarter suffices. I usually go by train and back same day, but the next time I go by car I will try to look you up — I shall not be much at home during the Commercial Show as I am busy finding routes for a motor trial and have to report on the 11th....." from which one concludes that Katherine was, as in the past, given to inaccurate statements and that Lionel was becoming more and more actively involved in the administration and organisation of motor sport!

Despite the great financial depression that had so clouded the closing years of the decade and which was to send Great Britain off the Gold Standard, it would seem that Martin's financial affairs had not suffered irretrievably, though it must be admitted that he was no longer saddled with the sort of expenses that had befallen him in the Bamford & Martin days. After the collapse of his Company's affairs in 1925, Lionel and his family continued to live at 'The Hollies', Pembroke Villas, Kensington, but early in 1932 they moved to 'Palings', Warboys Road, Kingston-on-Thames, Surrey, a house which, particularly when furnished as luxuriously as it was could not have been the home of anyone in 'reduced circumstances', as the genteel phrase of the time had it. Of 'Palings' when she knew it, Mrs Gripper remarks; "'Palings' was sumptuously furnished in very good taste and did give the impression of gracious living. Kate's bedroom was beautifully furnished, fitted cupboards etc., and lovely covers and curtains made by Kate herself....."

1932 saw Martin, in his capacity as an RAC Steward, involved in one of the most sensational and controversial race finishes that ever occurred at the track. This was at the conclusion of the British Empire Trophy Meeting at Brooklands after a grand tussle between John Cobb in the big V-12 Delage and George Eyston in the single-seater record-breaking 8-litre sleeve-valve Panhard. Cobb had crossed the line, winning the 100-mile race at a speed of 126.363mph with Eyston in the Panhard right on his tail with an average for the race of 126.354mph. Friends of Eyston persuaded him to lodge a protest on the grounds that Cobb had baulked him earlier in the race, an appeal which was upheld. This decision left Cobb with no other option than to appeal to the RAC. Lionel Martin, S.C.H. Davis and Sir Algernon Guinness were appointed to sift the evidence. The Hon. Ewen Montagu represented Cobb and Ernest Hancock represented Eyston and the result of this "truly

135

legal meeting'', as Boddy puts it in his *History of Brooklands,* was that the earlier decision was reversed and the race awarded to Cobb by one-fifth of a second, or 0·14mph.

On a lighter note, perhaps, it is said that Lionel was asked to testify when the validity of the will of the late Montagu Napier, an old friend from Bath Road days, was being challenged in a court of law on the grounds that Napier's eccentricity amounted to an alleged invalidation of the will's bequests. Napier, it seems, had a strong aversion to carrying any luggage when travelling and would never take more luggage with him when on tour than literally a toothbrush. At any hotel at which he stayed the night he would send out the 'Boots' with instructions to go and buy him a pair of pyjamas and any other things he might need. These would be left at the hotel in the morning when Napier moved on. At intervals, if his travels lasted that long, when Napier would have been expected to need clean shirts or underwear, the 'Boots' would be told to go out and buy replacements, the old ones then being discarded. When questioned if he knew of these habits of Napier's, Martin replied in the affirmative and further, that he considered such behaviour perfectly reasonable, adding that if he himself could afford to do so he would act in exactly the same way!

January 1933 found Lionel and Katherine Martin both venturing abroad again in motor competition, this time in the famous Monte Carlo Rally which had been won for the first time by a British car and driver in 1926 by the Hon. Victor Bruce with an A.C., the same Victor Bruce who had driven the early Aston-Martin 'Coal Scuttle' in the very first 200-Miles Race at Brooklands. Martin, of course, loved Continental motoring and was widely experienced in it. For the 1933 Monte Carlo event Martin teamed up with two other co-drivers with a Humber Snipe 80 Sports Saloon, registered KV 3449, while Katherine Martin, with Mrs A.G. Gripper and Miss Barbara Marshall formed the all-woman crew of a Hillman 'Wizard' Sports Saloon, registered KV 3276. Kate, as was her way, christened the Hillman 'The Gizzard', but that is by the way! Both the Humber and the Hillman started from John o'Groats and a short account of the early stages of the event as seen by these two entrants was published in the Rootes House Magazine *Modern Motoring* in February 1933. A much more full and personal account of the Humber's part in the event was written by Martin himself and appeared in the next month's issue of that journal, but perhaps for the most personal account of any one may again refer to Mrs Gripper's comments to the author written so many years later.

She writes: ''.....actually we only had the usual 'odd spots of trouble' except for one thing. Just outside Le Mans, in the cold grey dawn, the exhaust pipe came loose and was too near the underpart of the car, which caught fire, with smoke pouring up through the back seat. Without a second thought Kate gets hold of the fire extinguisher, starts it going, but leaning over from the front seat. The result was she got most of the fumes and passed completely out. We had a good laugh about it afterwards but at the time it wasn't funny. Miss Marshall and I had to pull Kate out very rapidly and put her on the grass verge, at that time frozen solid and covered in snow. But Kate recovered fairly quickly in the fresh air, and though feeling a bit queer she insisted that we start off again at once. When we arrived at Le Mans for breakfast we others had the usual coffee and rolls but Kate preferred a double brandy at about 6.30 in the morning. Such was her nature — she had plenty of guts and would never give in. And so we journeyed on and had a great time in Monte Carlo and got the John o'Groats Ladies Cup....."

In the autumn of 1931 Lionel Martin, accompanied by his son John and one Henry Gadsby, a stockbroker, who was to navigate, had taken an earlier Hillman 'Wizard' Sports Saloon for an extended and testing run on the Continent, a tour that embraced no fewer than sixteen of the major Alpine Passes, including the Stelvio, the Galibier, the Furka and the Albula Passes, in a journey of some 2,250 miles during a period of ten days. On the Col du Parpaillon which rises to 8,600 feet, the party which by now included a fourth member found the going extremely difficult. The road was very narrow and poorly surfaced and abounded in extremely tight turns that necessitated several reverses to get round. But worse was to come; the tunnel at the summit was closed by huge iron doors at each end and at the far end one of the massive iron bolts had rusted up solid. It took the superhuman efforts of all three male members (for Gadsby's wife Sheila joined the party for the return trip) to prise it loose and get through. Martin wrote an account of this trip in *Modern Motoring* for November 1931.Perhaps this trip was an intentional overture for the Monte Carlo trip to be undertaken in 1933 and already described, or Martin may even have had in mind the further Continental competitions that he and Katherine were to undertake in the near future.

Be that as it may, it was for John Martin his first Continental motor tour — "a sort of minor Grand Tour" as he says of it — and he found the experience full of enchantment and one which gave him a lasting delight in motoring in Europe, while for the Hillman, the object was to test the car in conditions conducive to fuel vaporisation and John Martin and the rest of the crew carried out careful tests and temperature readings at the bottom, the half-way point and the summit of each of the many passes they climbed.

Neither the Humber Snipe 80 nor the two Hillman Wizards had been the Martins' personal cars for the second M.G. 18/80 had given place to an early Wolseley Hornet and this was to be the precursor of a 'run' of varying models of this type — no fewer than eight of them, mostly open-bodied sports tourers. It was in one of these, registered PJ 6061, that Lionel and Katherine entered for the International Alpine Trial of 1932, sharing the driving between them. They must have enjoyed the experience even though it involved taking part in what was acknowledged to be one of the toughest tests that a production car could be submitted to. Competition was truly international, and in the early to mid-'Thirties British cars of the calibre of Frazer Nash and Talbot 105 put up some outstanding performances. The Wolseley Hornet did not aspire to the same kind of markets as did either the Talbot or the Frazer Nash but was a popular sports car of the time in the low- to medium-price range.

In the following year, 1933, Mr and Mrs Martin were again competing in the Alpine Trial, this time in a Humber 'Twelve' Sports Tourer registered KV 5681, fitted, to use Martin's own words when describing the event in *Modern Motoring* for September 1933, with "a natty little open four-seater body painted green....." Two 'proving trips' with the car were undertaken prior to the event iself, one a trip to the Scottish Highlands, the other to the mountains of Wales which took in the course of what Martin describes as 'an important reliability trial'. Mention of the Scottish Highlands serves as a reminder that Martin, incidentally, was a keen fisherman, renting a beat on Loch Awe in pre-Great War days and later in life often fishing on the Broadlands estate of the late Lord Louis Mountbatten.

The Humber was even less a market rival to such as Talbots and Frazer Nashes than had been the Wolseley Hornet of the previous year, being a side-valve touring car dressed in the sporting manner, but the Martins enjoyed a trouble-free run in the Trial and gained the coveted "Plaquette souvenir de la Coupe des Alpes".

On British soil these years were active ones too, though here Lionel Martin confined his activities to administration, surveying routes, marshalling and as in the past, acting as Steward at the major motoring events at Brooklands and elsewhere. From September 1932 until the outbreak of war in 1939 he never missed a single Shelsley Walsh meeting, at all of which he acted as a Steward. Perusal of the motoring publications of the time will often reveal references to these activities on his part and his portly and easily recognisable form may be discerned in some of the illustrations in the motoring weeklies.

Katherine, however, was still actively participating as a driver and, for example, was the first to ascend the hill at the Shelsley meeting of 29 May 1933 in one of the 'run' of Wolseley Hornets that the Martins had about this time. Her times on this occasion were 68.0 secs on her first run which she improved to 64.8 on the second.

An amusing incident occurred when, around 1935, Lionel owned a Railton saloon which, as he did with so many of his cars, he took for extended Continental tours. For some years Martin had an 'official' part in the series of Alpine Trials as a senior member of the RAC, representing British interests and seeing that the British entrants and their cars were well looked after from an organisational point of view. While thus engaged with the Railton saloon and while motoring along the route of the Trial he was surprised and amused to hear the impressive whine of a high-powered supercharged Mercedes-Benz coming up astern accompanied by an unnecessary degree of loud horn-blowing and every sign of an impatient and self-important driver. Recognising in his mirror that the car behind him was that of the German Reichminister of Sport, Korpsführer Huhnlein, Martin derived considerable satisfaction from making full use of the Railton's phenomenal acceleration to outdistance his impatient pursuer. Ironically it was Martin who was appointed, a year or two later on the occasion of the 1938 British Grand Prix at Donington when the Mercedes-Benz and Auto-Union teams demonstrated so shatteringly their massive domination in the Grand Prix field, to drive General Huhnlein round the course in a Bentley prior to the race. One wonders whether Huhnlein was aware of the identity of his driver as being the same man who had so easily deflated his self-importance on a previous occasion, and one cannot help wondering if Martin, beneath his usual impeccable good manners did not permit himself a chuckle or two. Incidentally, Martin praised the Railton in an advertisement that was reproduced in a Railton catalogue.

The Railton saloon was followed by a brace of BMWs, cars whose performance in the more modern idiom of the late 'Thirties cannot fail to have impressed Martin at Brooklands, Donington, Shelsley and other events in this country and also in the Alpine Trials with which he had been so much concerned. While on a visit to America Martin purchased a Chevrolet in New York, drove it across the States to Hollywood where he went to visit his old schoolfriend Lionel Pape, the actor, and sold it on the western seaboard for more than its New York purchase price.

The outbreak of war in 1939 of course brought immediate restrictions on motor sport and on motoring, restrictions that soon worsened until only those with essential transport needs could obtain petrol at all. Martin was one of the members of a Main Committee of the BARC who met on 14 November 1939 to discuss the future of the Club vis-à-vis the wartime occupation of the Track. He was also one of a sub-committee empowered to elect honorary members for as long as hostilities might last.

Martin was by now over sixty years of age, but he saw in the restrictions on motoring an ideal opportunity to return to his old love, cycling. *The Bath Road News* of May 1940 reported a chance encounter between one of their senior members and Lionel Martin in Richmond Park one evening in that Spring. Martin was then riding a Raleigh and the two old cyclists talked for a while of the sort of things dear to the hearts of cycling clubmen. The Bath Road writer concluded by remarking: "We shall be surprised if his genial presence will not be in evidence at some of our road events and at our annual dinner....."

And so it was — force of circumstances, perhaps, but certainly not without genuine pleasure on Martin's part, had turned the wheel full circle. Some seven or eight months later *The Bath Road News* was able to report: "Lionel Martin has returned to the fold, and although he has only been in training for about a month or so, recently put in a ride of 100 miles. He has a bicycle as well as a tricycle.....in a recent letter to the Secretary he expresses his great pleasure at being re-elected as Vice President......"

Two further *Bath Road News* entries for February and June 1942 reveal the following: ".....For a change Martin clipped somebody else's wings. We understand that at the North Road Dinner he imbibed so freely that in reversing his car he bent up the wings of a North Roader's car!....." which may or may not be an argument for using a bike instead of a car in wartime; and in the second extract, in which is reported the Bath Road Club's Jubilee "50" event — ".....Lionel, tip-toeing through the tea-cups in the early hours, endeavouring to make as little noise as possible, succeeded in knocking over a pile of tin trays, stepped back into the bucket, sat in the sink, and dropped a couple of aitches....."

Martin had for very many years been a sufferer from diabetes and was supposed to be careful over his diet. His son John, however, recalls an occasion when the family spent much time solemnly testing wines with a hydrometer in order to ascertain which would be least harmful to him, but he himself preferring if need be a short life and a merry one to the dullness of such restrictions, joined in this somewhat farcical process knowing full well that he would continue as before. Ever since early manhood he had suffered bouts of illness and in 1943 was very seriously ill, his recovery at one stage being in doubt. *The Bath Road News* reported in its issue for November/December 1944 that "Lionel Martin's keenness and enthusiasm for the Club's well-being is a by-word. His serious illness of last year has not impaired his powers; in fact, we are told he rode up Reigate Hill recently; no mean performance....."

His support for the Bath Road Club was indeed outstanding. He frequently made generous gifts to it in money or kind or helped individual members under the cloak of anonymity, as well as turning out for events more rigorously than many a younger man. It is understandable, however, that anyone not used to the traditions of the Bath Road and similar long-established cycle clubs might find in a man of his maturity that such an absorbing interest was a little tiresome. Mrs Gripper remarks: "In the last few years of his life he took to the bicycle again, and became rather boring on the subject. The last time we had lunch there we had to go out and admire his new machine, 'head down, bottom up' type! while he rode it round the garden and he was really quite childish about the whole thing....."

Mrs Gripper continues later, "I know Kate was a bit nervous about him riding a tricycle at his age....." and, indeed, in 1944 he was knocked off his machine and badly injured. *The Bath Road News* reported, ".....We mentioned briefly in a previous issue that Lionel Martin was in hospital as the result of a cycling accident. Since then we have had the opportunity to visit him at Kingston Hospital and are glad to report that his broken thigh bones are rapidly mending. Lionel said, and this we think is typical of the man, 'I made up my mind to be cheerful whilst lying in bed' and believe it or not, he said, 'I'll get on my trike once I'm invalided home!'.

And this indeed he eventually did. Lt-Col. R.E.C. Jennings recalls Martin coming to stay near Reading where Col. Jennings then was and arriving on a racing tricycle! "Bath Road" Martin to the last!

Sadly, to the last it was. On Sunday 14 October 1945 Martin was riding his tricycle home when he was knocked down at the traffic lights at Gloucester Road, Kingston, not far from his home. He had an operation in Kingston County Hospital but died there on 21 October 1945, exactly a week after his accident.

More than a quarter of a century after Lionel Martin's death it is significant to be able to record the following impressions of him from those who knew him at first-hand.

From the late Lord Thomas of Remenham, DFC.

"I knew Lionel Martin and his lively wife 'Calamity' Kate very well. I liked his enquiring approach and his courage. It is fifty years ago, but in my mind's eye I can still see Lionel Martin at Brooklands wearing a waterproof black poncho smock, loosely belted and buttoned tightly round the neck and wrists, surmounted by what was cheekily called a 'gor blimey' cap and dandified by a vivid neckscarf. He still exuded dignity and good cheer because of his graceful movements and innate charm.

He — and his wife Kate — were almost founder members of the exclusive body of Brooklands that made the oval steeply-banked track the centre of post-1918 war motor sport development. It was the venue for enthusiastic amateurs and striving entrepreneurs who tried to find the formula for commercial success by pitting gaunt cockleshell contraptions against one another round the bumpy concrete.

Most fell by the pit-side. There was the Graham-White buckboard, the Crouch Carette driven by dentist Mr Moss, father of Stirling Moss, the G.N. Spider (its name the initials of Godfrey and Nash, its sponsors), there was the Enfield-Allday, the Calthorpe and others that have gone to the limbo. But Lionel Martin had financial muscle. His money came from China Clay pits in Cornwall and he had enough of it to give solid support to his hobby of producing a well-engineered and substantial small car. But while other people who were trying to pull themselves into the motor trade proper found their shoe-laces too light, Lionel Martin persisted for two years and more until at last even the sturdier boot-straps of the clay pits gave out and he had to cease 'going it alone'. He was hurt because, with all his modesty, he wanted to see his own name on the radiator badge of an established car. How the 'Aston-Martin' came about is interesting. There were two speed hill-climb events known as Aston Rowant and Aston Clinton. Lionel liked the euphony of the titles and found Aston-Martin had the same rhythm.

It never was a mass-production model and to-day when factory sizes are beginning to show that 'small is beautiful' rather than indicate that the giant complexes are stable, the original aim of Lionel Martin to create a select number of thoroughbreds has much to be respected."

From S.C.H. Davis

"Lionel Martin was a character rarely found in these days of ours. He was out and out an Etonian, perfect of manners, certain what was right and what was wrong in life as in all other things and a perfectionist if ever there was one.....In years far back he would have been a 'Dandy' but a dandy who knew how to work. I never knew him criticise a rival manufacturer savagely, always his manners were excellent. And to him, I think, each car had personality and an animal quality, so should be looked after all the time. If he thought a driver-owner mishandled his machine he left him in no doubt of his feelings.

Yes, he had real character."

From Lt-Colonel R.E.C. Jennings, MBE, DL., Formerly Editor of the 'Motor'.

"His love of good food, good wine and good living.....his great charm and kindness and wonderful old-world manners made a great impression on me."

From Capt. G.E.T. Eyston, OBE, MC.

"Lionel was an old Etonian and a very likeable character.....a true sportsman."

From Capt. The Revd Herbert Ward

"I remember him as a genial and bustling individual, very proud of the old school and modest about his successes with the Singer at Aston Clinton and elsewhere......Lionel Martin and C.S. Rolls make an oddly assorted pair of Old Etonians. Neither Harrow nor Winchester appear to have produced anyone to compare with them".

From 'The Bath Road News' of November/December 1945:

".....Of the man himself it is difficult to write; enthusiastic about his own cycling, he was equally enthusiastic in helping others. For instance, knowing that I had the greatest difficulty in financing my racing efforts, he was most generous in lending me bicycles, tricycles, tyres, etc., and in helping me in other ways, and I wasn't the only one he helped. Only recently he took considerable trouble to secure a tricycle for a very famous old-time rider who had become rather a cripple, and finally lent him a tricycle of his own. He also did a lot of good work for the Club behind the scenes, of which most members never heard. He was always cheerful, even in adversity....."

And of the cars themselves:

From a former owner, Lt-Colonel C.E. Bowden:

"I had a beautiful little cloverleaf Bamford Aston (in my view the prettiest of the Bamfords) in 1926 when stationed at York. It never gave the slightest trouble of any kind whatsoever. Of all the many types of car I have owned, I still think of my cloverleaf Bamford with its quiet side-valve engine and speedy travel and litle fuss as the nicest car I had ever owned. Lionel Martin evidently had ideas of quality production and design far above any other light car producer of his day.....and probably of to-day as well, in my view."

"They were in every way excellent cars with refinement, good road-holding, good brakes, good lines, and respectable performance from the 35bhp 1½-litre side-valve engine. They were also extremely expensive." (i)

"The customer who cared to pay nearly £800 for a 12hp light car was, however, rewarded for his taste by the exquisite quality of that car which generally, although the engine produced a mere 35bhp at 4000rpm, combined a fuel consumption of 35mpg with a maximum of over 70mph, and offered exceptional road-holding for a small British car.....and the refinement of all detail work rendered it almost the native equivalent of a Bugatti; it was, in fact, in spite of its rather homely design, capable of giving the Brescia a good run and frequently beat it in speed trials and hill-climbs." (ii)

(i) The Batsford Guide to Vintage Cars: Cecil Clutton, Paul Bird, Anthony Harding: Batsford, 1959, 1976.

(ii) The Vintage Motor Car: Cecil Clutton, John Stanford: Batsford, 1954.

APPENDIX 1

WORKS DRAWINGS
RELATING TO THE ROBB AND STRASBOURG OHC CARS

Component	Dates of Drawings	
Crankcase	18.2.1921	Robb single ohc engine
	21.2.1921	
	13.5.1922	Strasbourg engine
	23.10.1923	Mk.III engine
Sump	18.2.1921	Robb single ohc engine
	25.4.1922	Strasbourg engine
	23.10.1923	Mk.III engine
Cylinder block	4.2.1922	Strasbourg engine
Timing case	6.2.1922	,, ,,
Timing Diagram	8.2.1922	,, ,,
Cylinder block	9.2.1922	,, ,,
General Arrangements		
Block/Head	13.2.1922	,, ,,
Engine complete	22.2.1922	,, ,,
Mk.III	20.2.1924	Mk.III engine

(ctsy: N.F. Murray)

As will be seen from the above, the bulk of the drawings for the engine components for the TT (or Strasbourg) cars were not completed until February 1922, a bare five months before the race itself. The new engines had to be built and tested in time to meet this target, a formidable task for the handful of men at 53 Abingdon Road, who had other commitments to the track cars and 'Bunny' that would be active during the coming season.

APPENDIX 2

GENERAL DATA FOR SIDE-VALVE CARS

Bore — 66·5mm   Stroke — 107mm
Cubic capacity — total swept volume 1487cc.
Cylinder capacity $= \text{T.S.V.}/4 = 371\cdot75\text{cc.}$
Piston area — 21·386 sq.ins.
BHP — Max. 45.   Max. piston speed 2·808 ft/sec
Rated HP (RAC) — 11
Max. torque — 58.5lbs/ft at 4000 r.p.m.
BMEP — 948 lbs.sq.in.   BHP per in^2 of piston area — 2·11
BHP per ton — 54   BHP per litre — 30
Compression ratios: approx 5·5 : 1 — 5·8 : 1
Stroke/Bore ratio: 1·61
Clutch: Hele-Shaw   Multi-plate   15 plates
Material: bronze & steel alternative

Gearbox	Ratios	Standard	Alternate
	1st	14 - 1	10·5 - 1
	2nd	7·2 - 1	6·2 - 1
	3rd	5·1 - 1	4·5 - 1
	4th	4 - 1	3·5 - 1
	R	14 - 1	10·5 - 1

Tooth pitch — (circular) ·375in.
Rear axle: ratios   3/1   3·2/1   3·5/1   3·75/1   4/1
Tooth pitch — according to ratio
Dry weight — 3 seater   16cwts.
Maximum speed in touring trim — 77 mph.
Brooklands lap speed guaranteed 65mph average
Fuel tank capacity — 8-9 gallons   oil capacity 9 pints
Fuel consumption — 35-45 mpg.   Oil consumption — 2000mpg
Wheels — Sankey steel, and later Rudge Whitworth — 710×90

APPENDIX 3

CARS OWNED BY LIONEL MARTIN

12/14 Clement-Bayard
28/30 Mors, Roi des Belges
20/30 Renault
35/45 Renault (open)
8 De Dion Victoria
8 De Dion 4-seater
45 Napier (open)
55 Napier (open)
12hp De Dion 4-cyl open 4-seater
12hp De Dion single-cyl.coupé
Siddeley-Deasey open 4-seater
Metallurgique Victoria 2-seat
1910 Sunbeam open 4-seater
     Sunbeam open 4-seater
1911 Star
     6hp De Dion 2-seater
1914 Singer (open)
     Singer coupé
     Calthorpe open 2-seater
1920 Peugeot open 2-seater
     Singer coupé
     Peugeot open 2-seater
     Singer ('Yellow Peril') open 2-seater
     30/98 Vauxhall open 4-seater
     Rolls-Royce open 4-seater (orange)
     Nazzaro open 4-seater
     Rolls-Royce 1914 Demo
     Rolls-Royce 1915 Demo
     Buick open 4-seater
     Buick all-weather
     Buick saloon
     Rolls-Royce open 4-seater (green)
     Rolls-Royce saloon (grey)
     Bugatti 2-seater
     Bugatti (Grand Prix)

Bugatti 2-seater
Rover 12 open 4-seater
Rover 12hp saloon
Austin Twenty all-weather
Aston-Martin original 2-seater
Aston-Martin cloverleaf
Aston-Martin 4-seater (red)
Aston-Martin 4-seater (ex-Rubin)
Riley Monaco 9hp saloon
Riley 9hp (open)
MG 18/80 fabric saloon
MG 18/80 coachbuilt saloon
Wolseley Hornet (original: PL25)
Wolseley Hornet, open, Abbey fabric
Wolseley Hornet Alpine (Daytona)
Wolseley Hornet open 2-seater (ex Abbott)
Wolseley Hornet 1934 open Daytona
Wolseley Hornet saloon 1934 (ex-Abbott)
Wolseley Hornet 1935 open Daytona
Wolseley Hornet 1935 saloon
Hillman Minx Show Model
Talbot 105 saloon
Railton saloon
BMW 45 cabriolet
BMW 55 Arnold saloon
Chevrolet (while in U.S.A.)
Lancia Aprilia
Lancia Aprilia
Fiat 508cc (Topolino)
Fiat 10/12 saloon

INDEX

150

PICTURE CREDITS

The Author is pleased to acknowledge with gratitude that the photographs appearing in this book have kindly been provided as under:

S.D. Wicks, Esq. (Frontispiece), The Provost and Fellows of Eton (1), *Cycling* (2, 5), The Bath Road Club (3, 4, 6), the late F.E. Ellis, Esq. (7, 8, 17, 19, 20, 22, 28, 47, 58), John Martin, Esq. (9, 10, 11, 12, 16, 18, 21, 24, 25, 30, 32, 33, 34, 35, 36, 37, 38, 39, 41, 44, 46, 48, 57, 59, 70, 86, 87, 91, 92, 93, 94), *The Autocar* (13, 14, 15, 83), S.C.H. Davis, Esq. (23), H.G. Conway, Esq. (26), The Brooklands Society (27), P.T. Beardsell, Esq. (29, 60, 80), R. Dallas Brett, Esq., OBE (31), W. Boddy, Esq. (40), The Aston Martin Owners Club (42), Mrs M. Morgan/N.F. Murray, Esq. (43, 49, 50, 73), The Vintage Sports Car Club Ltd. (45), the late Col. Clive Gallop/N.F. Murray, Esq. (51, 52, 53, 54, 55, 56), S. Maslin, Esq. (61), W.D. Hall, Esq. (62), W.H. Summers, Esq. (63, 64, 66, 67, 68, 69), Capt. The Revd H. Ward (65), the late Lt-Col. Charles Archdale (71), Marshall, Harris & Baldwin Ltd. (72, 81, 95), The Midland Automobile Club (74, 75, 90), D. Irvine, Esq./Mrs G. Ahern (76, 77, 78), Mrs A.G. Gripper (79, 88, 89), Guy Griffiths, Esq. (82), J.D. Hall, Esq. (84), T.A. Roberts, Esq., OBE (85)